Jacques Tati (center) in the company of two of his comic heroes, Buster Keaton (left) and Harold Lloyd (right).

Jacques TATI

a guide to references
and resources

A
Reference
Publication
in
Film

Ronald Gottesman
Editor

Jacques TATI

a guide to references and resources

LUCY FISCHER

G.K. HALL & CO.

70 LINCOLN STREET, BOSTON, MASS.

Library of Congress Cataloging in Publication Data

Fischer, Lucy.
  Jacques Tati, a guide to references and resources.

  Includes indexes.
  1. Tati, Jacques. I. Title.
PN1998.A3T32   016.79143′0233′0924   82-3112
ISBN 0-8161-8000-8   AACR2

This publication is printed on permanent/durable acid-free paper
MANUFACTURED IN THE UNITED STATES OF AMERICA

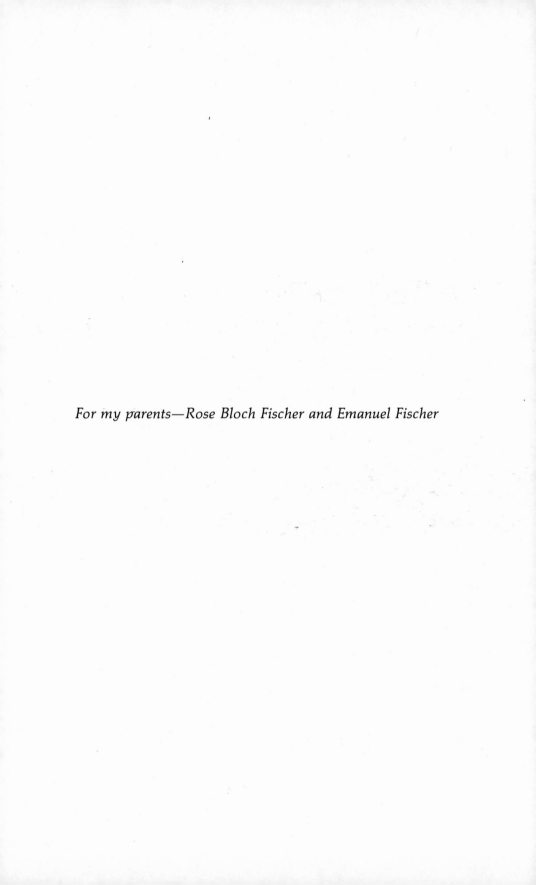

For my parents—Rose Bloch Fischer and Emanuel Fischer

Contents

The Author

Lucy Fischer received her Ph.D. in Cinema Studies from New York University. She has written extensively on film for such publications as Film Quarterly, Sight and Sound, Cinema Journal, Quarterly Review of Film Studies, Millenium Film Journal and Wide Angle and several of her articles have appeared in museum catalogues and anthologies on the cinema. Ms. Fischer worked for several years in a curatorial capacity at The Museum of Modern Art in New York City, and the Museum of Art, Carnegie Institute in Pittsburgh. Presently, she directs the Film Studies Program at the University of Pittsburgh.

Preface

I first became aware of the films of Jacques Tati as a sophomore in high school, when my French teacher, Miss Block, suggested that we go to see Mon oncle which was then playing to rave reviews in New York City. The title, somehow, made me think that the film was for "children," and, being more smug then than I am now, I did not go. In retrospect, I wish that I had listened to Miss Block and had become aware of the joys of Tati at an earlier stage of my life.

As it was, I did not become familiar with Tati's work until 1973 when Playtime opened in New York City. I recall going to see it with a friend on a summer Sunday afternoon. From the moment the film began, we were both amused and enchanted by the film's strange comic tone. Though most of the audience was clearly nonplussed, our lone shrieks of laughter filled the hall. It was that screening of Playtime that stirred my interest in Tati. Later, as a doctoral candidate at New York University, I wrote a dissertation on his films, which now forms the basis of the critical essay in Chapter II.

Research on Tati presents some special difficulties. Not all of his films are in American distribution nor preserved in archives. Therefore, it is impossible to see his early short films here or his latest work Parade. Published sources of information on Tati also evince problematic gaps. Biographies are frequently sketchy and lacking in historical detail. Credits for his early films often fail to specify such things as running time or cast of characters. In such cases, the best published data available have been combined to provide the most complete information possible.

Research for the annotated bibliography (Chapter IV) was based on an examination of all important film journals catalogued in major libraries: The Museum of Modern Art Film Study Center; UCLA Theater Arts Library; New York Public Library (Research Branch); American Film Institute Library; Film Section, Carnegie Institute; Lincoln Center Library of the Performing Arts; University of Southern California Library; and the French Film Office. European libraries were also contacted. The choice of film reviews was dictated largely by the availability of such articles in library clipping files or

Preface

indexed periodicals.

Articles in Chapter IV have been annotated in considerable detail, since much of the material on Tati is in French and frequently
difficult to locate. In those cases where articles have not been
personally annotated, they have been listed with the source of their
bibliographic citation. Those interested in pursuing additional articles on Tati in French publications of a more general orientation
should consult the bibliographies of Cauliez (entry 192) and Agel
(entry 62). Major interviews with Tati have been both annotated and
listed in the "Interviews" section of Chapter V.

For the archival section of the book (Chapter VI), all members
of the Fédération Internationale des Archives du Film were surveyed,
as well as many FIAF "observers." Those listed have responded af-
firmatively with information concerning film or print material on
Tati. Institutions that claim to have no relevant material have not
been included.

Obviously, a research project of this type depends on the aid of
countless colleagues and institutions in the field. I would first
like to thank certain faculty members at New York University who
worked with me on the thesis: Professors Noël Carroll, Jay Leyda,
Robert Sklar, William Everson, William Rothman, and, most particularly, William Simon.

My research was facilitated by the staff members of various film
libraries and archives. At The Museum of Modern Art, Charles Silver,
Emily Sieger, Ron Magliozzi, Eileen Bowser, Jon Gartenberg, and Bob
Summers helped me on the project. At the Pacific Film Archives, I
am grateful to Nancy Goldman, and at the UCLA Theater Arts Library,
to Audree Malkin and Edith Moore. Debbie Boutchard assisted me at
the American Film Institute Resource Center, and the staff of the
Lincoln Center Library of the Performing Arts was extremely cooperative (particularly Carol Garner). Jillian Slonim of the French Film
Office provided me access to important clipping files.

I am also indebted to several colleagues in Pittsburgh who gave
me assistance on the project. Robert Haller (former director of
Pittsburgh Film-Makers) provided me the opportunity to lecture on
Tati on two occasions in 1979. Geralyn Huxley of the Film Section,
Carnegie Institute, helped research film distributors and prepare
the index. Marcia Landy, Dana Polan, and Bill Judson of the
University of Pittsburgh kindly read sections of the critical essay
and offered their comments. Donie Durieu and Channa Weyel generously
helped with French translation and Mariolina Salvatori assisted in the
annotation of Italian publications. I am also grateful to the secre-
tarial staff of the Department of English at the University of
Pittsburgh for typing the final manuscript in the midst of their
other work.

Preface

I would also like to thank Ernest Callenbach, Susan Defosset, and Barbara Durham of the University of California Press for allowing "M. Hulot et le temps" by André Bazin to be translated and published in the text. It is a pivotal essay on Tati and its availability in English, as translated by Walter Albert, makes a contribution to the field of Tati scholarship.

I am indebted to Ron Gottesman, who served as a supportive and patient editor of this project and helped me locate certain source materials. I would also like to thank Karin Kiewra for her editorial work on the text.

Several friends in the field were thoughtful enough to direct me to relevant materials and/or articles. I am thinking of Ellen Feldman, Stuart Liebman, Richard Peterson, Craig Johnson, Jonathan Rosenbaum, and, particularly, of Lindley Hanlon.

Finally, I would like to thank my husband Mark Wicclair, who has been most supportive of this project and has had to have a sense of humor equal to Tati's to see me through it.

January 1982

I. Biographical Background

Jacques Tati was born on 9 October 1908 at Pecq, France, a sub-urb of Paris. His family claimed a diverse ethnic heritage. His father, Emmanuel Tatischeff, was Russian--the son of Count Dmitri Tatischeff, the attaché to the Russian Embassy in Paris.[1] Tati's mother, Marcelle Van Hoof, was born in France, but her father was of Dutch extraction. One of Tati's grandmothers was Italian.

Tati's Dutch grandfather was a picture framer by profession and reputedly worked for such artists as Toulouse-Lautrec and Vincent Van Gogh.[2] Tati's father eventually joined him in business and opened an antique-picture-frame shop on Rue Caumartain in Paris which employed some thirty-five workers. Jacques attended the Lycée de Saint-Germain-en-Laye and, later, the Hanley Professional School at Choisy-le-Roi.[3]

Following his training, he joined his father in the picture-framing trade and prepared for entry into L'École Nationale Des Arts et Métiers. He did his military service in Saint Germain, at the bar-racks of the Place Royale, in the 16th Dragoons. Tati has said that his first "research" on comic effects grew out of his military experi-ence.[4]

At some point early on in his professional training, Tati went to England and served an apprenticeship to a picture framer named Spillers.[5] Evidently, however, he became more involved with the sport of rugby than he did with his craft. While in England, he played with the London Club of Westcome Park and, when he returned home, joined the Racing Club of France.[6]

MIME CAREER

Despite his father's attempts to steer him toward the family busi-ness, Tati resisted (although one might argue that his later career in the cinema is a transposition of the picture-framing trade).

Rather, Tati gravitated toward the theater--having discovered his
love of performance while executing postgame mimes for his rugby
teammates.

Evidently Tati's informal numbers frequently involved subjects
other than sports. As Alfred Sauvy (an old teammate) recalls, Tati
would often spontaneously perform comic scenes. Once, on the plat-
form of a bus, Tati imitated a radio commentary, providing political
editorials, commercials, songs, sports accounts, and so on. On other
occasions, he did imitations of painters or pianists.[7]

Tati's first public appearance occurred in 1931 at the Racing
Club Revue, a theatrical event staged annually by his rugby group.
It is not clear what numbers he performed in the 1931 revue, but
Sauvy recollects that one year Tati chose to represent, single-
handedly, an entire railroad station:

> Leaving by one door, in order to return, after a second,
> by another, dressed in a new indescribable costume
> . . . unravelling all the fauna of travellers: the
> grump, the gate-crasher, the fastidious traveller,
> the father of the family, the crazy one, etc.--all
> that in total silence.[8]

The positive response that Tati received from his audience awaken-
ed him to the possibilities of a theatrical comedy career. As he ex-
presses it:

> I began to feel the joys that my new profession furn-
> ished. I therefore took the long and arduous route
> of music-hall artists, going from city to city, from
> theatre to circus, from circus to cabaret.[9]

Tati's father was, however, decidedly unenthusiastic about his son's
unconventional vocational plans and threatened to cut him off "without a sou."[10] But Tati pursued his goal, though it had few financial
rewards. "When I needed to eat," he recalls, "I would go to a certain
cabaret and imitate a sloshed waiter. . . . For an evening of sloshed
waiting, I would be given dinner and fifty francs."[11]

From 1931 through 1933, Tati made the rounds of Parisian theatrical establishments without achieving much success. In 1933, he was
engaged by Louis Leplée at Gerny's where he performed a mime of a
restaurant maître d'hôtel. He went on to appear at the Théâtre Michel
and later recieved attention for his rendition of sports mimes at the
Ritz. The particular occasion for this latter engagement was a gala
celebrating the ocean liner Normandie's blue-ribbon award. Present
at the event were many celebrities of the day, including Maurice
Chevalier. In 1936, Tati was placed on a program at L'A.B.C. by
Mitty Goldin. Later in the same year he appeared at the Casino-de-
Brides les-Bains.[12]

Biographical Background

Few precise descriptions of Tati's sports mimes survive. Perhaps the best discussion occurs in Geneviève Agel's monograph, Hulot parmi nous. There she speaks of his boxing mime as involving a "tragic whirlwind of movement" and describes his head as moving like a boxer's punching bag.[13] She also recollects his piece, "Le Voyage en tramway" which depicts a man on a bus trying to get a seat, "his vest pulled by the crowd, a nosy person reading the newspaper over his shoulder."[14] Of the number, "La Partie de pêche," Agel recalls the various comic stages in Tati's mime of the amateur fisherman: "the joy of solitude, satisfaction of 'the preparation,' . . . optimistic expectation, uneasiness, distraction, nervousness, passivity . . . the hysteria of the catch."[15]

However, the most famous and glowing account of Tati's sports mimes comes in a journal of Colette dated 28 June 1936. She writes:

> Henceforth I believe that no festive, artistic, or
> acrobatic spectacle could equal the displays given by
> this astonishing man who has invented something which
> includes dance, sport, satire, and pageantry. He has
> created at the same time the player and the ball and
> the racket; the balloon and the person inflating it;
> the boxer and his adversary; the bicycle and the
> cyclist. His hands empty, he has created the acces-
> sory and the partner. His power of suggestion is that
> of a great artist . . . In Jacques Tati, horse and
> rider, all Paris will see, living, the fabulous
> mythical creature, the Centaur.[16]

Tati's experience as a vaudeville performer clearly influenced his later cinematic career. As a film comedian, he has always seen himself within the context of a tradition that had its roots in the stage. As Tati explains it:

> All film comics worthy of this name were first formed
> in the music-hall or circus. It is impossible to make
> a comic film without having learned one's craft "on the
> boards," in contact with the public. Otherwise one
> makes literary comedy.[17]

He speaks, as well, of how the music hall sensitized him to audience response. On the stage, he notes, "one must adapt himself each evening to a new public: little tradesmen, or 'chic' people, hairdressers or laborers, their different reactions . . ."[18]

Given the style of Tati's later films, it seems significant that his theatrical experience was that of a mime. For although it is a mistake to think of Tati's film technique as reminiscent of silent comedians (sound being a crucial element in his style), he does, nonetheless, minimize dialogue. Clearly, Tati's background as a mime informs his own performance mode, as well as his direction of other

3

actors in his films.

The precise subject of Tati's music-hall mimes also reveals a relationship to the style and content of his cinematic work. His concentration on sports mimes, per se, has various implications. First of all, Tati sees sports activity as preparatory for the comic art. As he has stated, "What one demands primarily of a comic actor is to have sports training."[19] Thus, by taking sports as his mime subject, Tati dramatizes the prerequisite activity for the comic craft itself.

The sports mimes are significant in yet other respects. As we shall see, one of the basic themes in Tati's cinematic work is the status of leisure in the contemporary world. Clearly, Tati's discourse on the issue of leisure begins with his sports mimes. From the descriptions that survive of those routines (which cite his imitation of the animated sports spectators as well as players), it would seem that for Tati sports represented a participatory form of leisure which has become less prevalent in the automated, technological world. Also relevant to this interest in leisure is the mime piece, "La Partie de pêche," which does not fall strictly within the sports catagory. For it does not seem a long way from this satire of the Sunday fisherman to the parody of summer vacationers in Les Vacances.

Aside from the concern with leisure, the mime pieces have other ties to Tati's later cinematic work. "Le Voyage en tramway," for example, involves what we might term a comedy of everyday situations, of groups of people in public places. This seems a forerunner of the comedy of observation that will characterize the beach-hotel world of Les Vacances, the Parisian neighborhoods of Mon oncle, the airport and restaurant of Playtime, and the highway locale of Trafic.

Moreover, one can see in Tati's various mime pieces specific foreshadowings of later cinematic vignettes. His early satire of radio commentary sparks associations with his parody of the medium in Les Vacances and Playtime. And his mime of a railroad station seems a forerunner of the opening sequence of Les Vacances. Finally his music-hall roles of maître d'hôtel and "sloshed waiter" seem ancestors of the distracted waiters in both Les Vacances and Playtime, and of the distraught maitre d' of the Royal Garden Restaurant.

SHORT FILMS/ACTING ROLES

At the same time that Tati launched a successful career as a cabaret performer, he began a parallel pursuit--the production of short comic films. Although Tati himself discounts the artistic merit of his early work, the shorts are worthy of consideration as steps in his evolution from music-hall performer to film director.[20]

His first effort was <u>Oscar, champion de tennis</u> (1932), which he
scripted, directed, and starred in, performing his tennis mime. This
particular sports piece was to reappear some twenty years later in
<u>Les Vacances</u>. <u>Oscar</u> was evidently of poor technical quality and, ac-
cording to Armand Cauliez, was never completed.[21]

In 1934, Tati wrote the script for <u>On Demande une brute</u> and decided to enlist two directors to supervise the film's production,
Charles Barrois and his assistant, René Clément. In the film, Tati
plays a henpecked husband, who, through a series of misunderstandings,
fights a wrestling match under the guise of being a champion.[22]
Claude Beylie, in an article on Tati's early cinematic work, says,
"The film marks the birth of an absolutely new comic character; clum-
sy, ungainly, reminiscent of a rope dancer, not knowing what to do
with his immense size . . ."[23]

Another short, <u>Gai dimanche</u>, directed by Jacques Berr, followed
in 1935. Again Tati scripted the work and appeared in the film along
with the famous clown, Rhum. According to Philip Strick, Tati appeared in the role of a "luckless dandy" who goes on a picnic with a salesman friend only to meet up with a series of mechanical and gastronomic
mishaps.[24] Evidently the film is interesting for its use of sound,
and certain sequences have been noted for their foreshadowing of the
audiovisual techniques of Tati's later work.[25]

In 1936, Tati scripted and appeared in <u>Soigne ton gauche</u> which
was directed by René Clément. This film again involved a reworking
of Tati's sports mimes, in this case, a boxing piece. According to
Cauliez, it is his best short film of the period, and Tati himself
concurs. "The fourth short film," he has remarked, "made me laugh
in the right way, so it was worth going on."[26]

In 1938, Tati produced, scripted, and appeared in <u>Retour à la</u>
<u>terre</u>, after which the war temporarily interrupted his cinematic
career. Although, as Philip Strick points out, the latter two films
were minor works, they did contain elements that were to reappear in
Tati's first feature film, <u>Jour de fête</u>: the use of location shooting and the character of a meddling postman.[27]

In general, Tati's early films of 1932-38 were poorly received,
and the director himself makes no claims for their aesthetic merit.
However, they are valuable as records of Tati's music-hall mimes, and
for providing insight into his evolution from cabaret performer to
film actor/director.

Along with his early cinematic ventures, Tati continued to perform
his music-hall act in various European countries. He toured
Scandinavia, Germany, Italy, and England, where he appeared at the
London Casino and Mayfair Hotel in 1936 and 1937. According to Jean
Quéval, Tati's tour was temporarily interrupted when he ran into prob-
lems involving another performer's theft of his material.[28] Shortly

before the war, Tati was in great demand and evidently performed in Berlin, where he appeared with Werner Fink.[29] In 1939, as Tati was about to continue his tour in America, he was drafted into the army and served in the infantry. When he was discharged, he spent time in Sainte-Sévère, Indre-et-Loire, the village that was later to serve as the setting for his first feature film, Jour de fête.

In May of 1944, Tati married Micheline Winter, and they subsequently had two children, Sophie and Pierre. Before resuming his directorial career, however, Tati appeared as an actor in two films by Claude Autant-Lara. His first and larger role was that of a ghost in the fantasy, Sylvie et le fantôme (1945). Tati plays the specter of a handsome young hunter killed a century ago in a duel. As an invisible ghost (rendered in superimposition), he wanders about his ancestral home, unseen by the young mistress of the estate, who has fallen in love with his portrait. This was clearly an uncharacteristic role for Tati, the music-hall comedian, though the grace and elegance of his performance benefited from his mime experience. However, as viewed from the vantage point of Tati's later filmic work, his performance in Sylvie takes on a special resonance. For in all his comic films, there exists a strain of unrequited romantic love--M. Hulot's tentative courtship of Martine in Les Vacances, his accidental "date" with Barbara in Playtime. Hulot's love is, however, always remote, idealized, and unfulfilled; as a lover he is more an ethereal ghost than a corporeal man. Tati next had a small role as a soldier in Autant-Lara's Le Diable au corps (1946). He appeared as part of a group of soldiers singing around a bar piano in celebration of the armistice.

The following year marked the beginning of Tati's serious directorial career in the cinema. He wrote the scenario for L'École des facteurs which was to be directed by René Clément. Clément fell ill, however, and Tati took over as the director and star of the film. L'École des facteurs was a comedy of French village life, and Tati took the role of François, the village postman.

FEATURE FILMS

After the release of L'École des facteurs in 1947, Tati decided to rework the film as a feature, hoping to increase its commercial potential. The film was retitled Jour de fête and released in 1949. In producing Jour de fête, Tati experimented on various technical fronts. He utilized magnetophone sound, a process that had scarcely been introduced at the time. He also shot one negative in the new Thomson-Color process and another safety negative in traditional black and white. Unfortunately, due to a laboratory error, the color negative was never printed, and Tati had to abandon the comic effects he sought to gain. Certain statements he has made, however, allow us to reconstruct what the color conception of Jour de fête may have involved. He speaks of the little town being "very black and white, dark . . . the only color [being] brought to it by the fairground, the merry-go-round, etc."[30]

Jour de fête was shot in 1947 at Sainte-Sévère over a six-month period and was financed by a cooperative society of which most of the crew were members.[31] When the film was completed, it was shown to a small private audience which liked the film but criticized its "tenuous" comic structure. Tati and his producer, Fred Orain, therefore, shot some additional gag material (for example, a sequence involving Francois's unwitting disruption of a mourning scene) and re-edited the film.[32]

At first, distributors rejected Jour de fête, and Tati and Orain decided to arrange a preview at a theatre in Neuilly. The reaction of the public was enthusiastic, and the release of the film was thereby assured. Its 1949 exhibition proved to be a critical success and established Tati as an important figure in French cinema. One critic said, in fact, that Jour de fête "incontestably . . . marked a date in the history of French film comedy."[33]

The film was a commercial success as well. A Variety article of 25 May 1949, in fact, touted it as a low-budget triumph. It states that it had cost only $30,000 to make and had already grossed some $12,000 in its first week of simultaneous release at four Paris first-run theaters.[34] In some ways, Tati's success as a filmmaker created renewed public interest in his work as a mime. And late in 1949, he gave a performance of his music-hall act at the Casino of Knokke-le-Zoute in Belgium.

After the success of Jour de fête, producers approached Tati to make sequels to the film based on the character of François. Typically, Tati refused this offer to crank out formula pictures and, instead, developed an idea he had for a more complex persona. As Tati recalls:

> It was then that I had the idea of presenting M. Hulot,
> personage of complete independence, of absolute indif-
> ference, . . . whose lack of attention, is his principal
> defect. [He is] in our functional era a maladapted
> person.[35]

Fortunately, the commercial success of Jour de fête allowed Tati to pursue his conception of Hulot and to make Les Vacances de Monsieur Hulot, the first film based on this comic character. It was made under financially independent conditions with the help of Fred Orain, his producer on Soigne ton gauche and Jour de fête. Filming began in the summer of 1951 at Saint-Mar-Sur-Mer in Brittany. Shooting was interrupted, however, by funding problems, which explains why the credits for the film often list several persons associated with the same production task.[36] After eight months of shooting, the film was completed in October of 1952. Following its French premiere, Tati made slight readjustments in the montage for its showing at the Cannes

Film Festival where it won the International Critics Prize of 1953.

Les Vacances was a commercial and critical success. Shot on a budget of under $215,000, it reputedly returned twice that amount during its first Paris run before becoming a popular success in the French countryside and abroad.[37] To publicize its exhibition in America, Tati came to the United States in November and June of 1954 and appeared on an NBC special, "Fanfare," performing his sports mimes.[38]

Following the success of Les Vacances, Tati began working on the script for his next film, Mon oncle. A serious automobile accident in 1955, however, held up work on the film until 1956.[39] Under the auspices of Spectafilm, (Tati's own production company, formed in 1956), Mon oncle was shot on location at Vieux-Saint-Maur and at the Victorine Studios in Nice. It was Tati's first realized color film and proved a great commercial success.[40] Mon oncle also received many honors, among them the Academy of Motion Picture Arts and Sciences' Oscar for the best foreign film of 1958. Following his acceptance of the award in 1959, Tati toured the United States.

In 1961, Tati rereleased Jour de fête and exhibited it in Paris in the form of a show entitled "Jour de fête à l'Olympia." In addition to screening the film, Tati appeared on stage performing various sports mimes: the goalkeeper, the fisherman, the tennis player, and finally, the cavalier and his mount.[41] Evidently he had the proscenium of the stage decorated with French village scenes and strung some garlands above the screen. The print of the film was stencil-colored in a manner reminiscent of turn-of-the-century color effects. Thus, such images as flags, balloons, and the red light of François's bicycle were highlighted, as they would have been had Jour de fête been released in color as planned.

Tati was not to make another film for some nine years; however, in the interim he did rerelease Les Vacances, adjusting the montage of certain sequences and altering the sound track.[42] Evidently it triumphed in a run on the Champs-Élysées.

During this period, Tati made plans to run a movie theater dedicated to the comic genre.[43] He changed the name of the Parisian Lux to Arlequin and opened with a rerelease of Jour de fête. In keeping with Tati's own philosophy of filmmaking, the theater was to be a place in which the spectator would reign supreme. As he himself stated, "The spectator was king there . . . reservation of seats by telephone, gentlemen in white gloves, polite and gentle usherettes, fanfares at the intermission."[44]

Also in this period, Tati (along with Raymond Rohauer) purchased Educational Films Company—a collection of some thousand shorts, including those of Mack Sennett. A Variety article of September 1964 reports that he and Rohauer had plans to re-edit and redistribute many

titles.[45] Evidently Tati's Arlequin project was abandoned when he
ran into copyright problems concerning the exhibition of silent
American films, particularly those of Buster Keaton, one of Tati's
admitted comic mentors.

Although the Arlequin project never reached fruition, it is significant for the way in which it displays Tati's concern for the history of film comedy. Tati has always seen his own comic persona within the context of a long line of film comedians. And it is telling
that his greatest thrill on his 1959 American tour was meeting Harold
Lloyd, Buster Keaton, Stan Laurel, and Mack Sennett.[46]

During this period following the making of Mon oncle, Tati's plans
were not, however, restricted to work on the Arlequin or to the rerelease of his prior films. Rather, he began working on the script
for Playtime, a document that would eventually exceed five hundred
pages.[47] It seems fitting that at the time of Playtime's conception
Tati was involved in reviewing his earlier films, for Tati's masterpiece can be seen as extending and exemplifying the themes and techniques of all his previous work.

Since the decor of Playtime would be that of a contemporary airport and modern office building, Tati thought, at first, to shoot at
Orly and in Paris. He soon realized, however, that on-location shooting would not allow him the rigorous control of the environment that
Playtime necessitated. Decor could not be precisely designed; and
the daily activities of those locales would lessen his control of the
shooting schedule and mise-en-scène. As Tati himself explains:

> For my construction we couldn't go to the Drugstore
> and Orly and stop work there, it would have been im-
> possible. And I wanted this uniformity: all the
> chairs, for instance, in the restaurant, in the
> back--they're all the same. The floors are the same,
> the paint's the same.[48]

Therefore, Tati made the bold decision to construct an extrava-
gant set for Playtime, a fabricated glass and steel city located at
Saint-Maurice that would affectionately be known as "Tativille."
In September 1964, bulldozing began and the foundations of buildings
were laid.[49] In the 1968 Cahiers du cinéma tribute to Playtime, critic Jean-André Fieschi catalogues the materials involved in this extraordinary filmic construction: 50,000 cubic meters of concrete;
4,000 square meters of plastic; 3,200 meters of timber; 1,200 square
meters of glass--a total of some 15,000 square meters.[50] Several
architects were hired for the project, which took eight months to
complete.[51]

Playtime involved some ten years of preparation and took three
years to film.[52] Because it was shot in 70mm and stereophonic sound,
the cost of production was prohibitive. Tativille alone added some

$800,000 to production costs, and the total expenditures amounted to over $3 million.[53] The film opened at a Parisian theater especially outfitted for the occasion.

Although Playtime was a critical triumph, it was a commercial disaster. Its radical stylistic conception, its monumental length, its lack of emphasis on Hulot, were clearly not consonant with popular tastes. Tati tried to salvage the film by cutting it by some fifteen minutes after its Parisian premiere, but it remained a box-office failure.[54] Tati wound up heavily in debt with his house mortgaged to cover expenses for the film.[55] The banks responded by impounding the rights to his work (Jour de fête, Les Vacances, Mon oncle, and Playtime). Therefore, Tati had no source of income, and the films were virtually absent from the world's commercial film circuit. Thus, he paid a heavy price for having staunchly maintained his independent artistic and financial status.

Tati, nonetheless, managed to raise enough money to make Trafic in 1971. A Franco-Italian coproduction, it was filmed in Holland. Following its American release, Tati toured the United States in 1972, making appearances at a festival in his honor in New Orleans, at a French film gala in Dallas, and at The Museum of Modern Art in New York City.[56]

In 1973, Tati recieved an invitation from Swedish television to create a program based on the theme of the circus. Shot in Stockholm on videotape, the piece was eventually transferred to film and released as Parade. With Parade, Tati came full circle to his theatrical roots. For the film includes a performance of such classic mime routines as the paunchy fighter, the prancing horse, the agitated tennis player, and the testy soccer goalie.[57]

It is significant that during this period of financial hardship at home, Tati sought international funding for both his projects and shot each outside of his native France. In 1974, his films were auctioned off in Paris, a circumstance bemoaned by the French film community.[58]

During this period, despite professional discouragement and bouts with serious illness, Tati began working on a script for a new film titled Confusion.[59] According to Brent Maddock, who has examined Tati's scenario, the film

> [would] be structured on Tati's typical riffing style.
> Hulot would appear . . . as an ingenious inventor
> hired by an enterprising American television network
> to install his new Hulot-color system in their news
> camera. Travelling about with the television news
> crew gives Hulot ample opportunity to create his
> brand of havoc or confusion in the most varied of
> locations.[60]

10

In 1975, an article appeared in the Hollywood Reporter stating that Confusion would be produced in the United States by David Frost and Paradine Productions.[61]   Later, a second article retracted that claim, noting that Confusion would be made in Europe.[62]   Then in February 1977, a New York Times article entitled "Jacques Tati and His Movies Return after Enforced Vacation" reported that Tati was once again working on the film.[63] His decision resulted from a Paris distributor's payment of some $1.6 million to the banks for the distribution rights to Tati's previous films.

In recent years, Tati's early work has been rereleased in Europe. Jour de fête opened in Paris in February of 1977 and was followed by the exhibition of Les Vacances, Mon oncle, Playtime, and Trafic.[64] With this renaissance of Tati's films in the European cinema, one hopes that M. Hulot's enforced "holiday" from the film world has finally come to an end.

NOTES

1. Armand J. Cauliez, Jacques Tati, p. 5 (entry 192).   Cauliez lists Tati's grandfather as the tsar's ambassador to Paris.

2. Cited in Charles Moritz, ed., Current Biography, p. 44 (entry 146) and in Cauliez, Tati, p. 5 (entry 192).

3. P. Guth, "J'ai vu Tati tourner son prochain film," p. 4, (entry 71).

4. Cauliez, Tati, p. 6 (entry 192).

5. Penelope Gilliatt, Jacques Tati, p. 10 (entry 292).   The sources are all very vague about the exact dates of Tati's departure or his return to France.

6. Jean Quéval, "Jour de fête," p. 165 (entry 21).

7. Alfred Sauvy, "Jacques Tati: Hier, aujourd'hui et demain," in Cauliez, Tati, p. 171 (entry 192).   Sauvy later collaborated with Tati on the scenario of On demande une brute.

8. Ibid., p. 172 (entry 192). My translation.

9. Tati in Cauliez, Tati, p. 6 (entry 192). My translation.

10. Tati in Gilliatt, Tati, p. 10 (entry 292).

11. Ibid.

12. Ibid., p. 18. The program for Tati's appearance at the Casino de Brides-les-Bains is shown in an illustration.

13. Geneviève Agel, Hulot parmi nous, p. 16 (entry 62). My translation.

14. Ibid. My translation.

15. Ibid. My translation.

16.   Colette, Le Journal, quoted in Agel, Hulot, pp. 16–17 (entry 62). My translation.

17.   Tati in Cauliez, Tati, p. 80 (entry 192). My translation.

18.   Ibid. My translation.

19.   Ibid. My translation.

20.   Jacques Tati in Penelope Gilliatt, "Profiles: Playing," p. 45 (entry 256).

21.   Cauliez, Tati, p. 7 (entry 192).

22.   Philip Strick, "Jour de fête," p. 49 (entry 152).

23.   Claude Beylie, "Tati inconnu," pp. 12–13 (entry 78). My translation.

24.   Strick, "Jour de fête," p. 49 (entry 152).

25.   Ibid.

26.   Tati in Gilliatt, "Profiles," p. 45 (entry 256).

27.   Strick, "Jour de fête," p. 49 (entry 152).

28.   Quéval, "Jour de fête," p. 165 (entry 21).

29.   Strick, "Jour de fête," p. 20 (entry 152).

30.   Tati in Harold G. Woodside, "Tati Speaks," p. 8 (entry 204).

31.   Quéval, "Jour de fête," p. 166 (entry 21).

32.   Strick, "Jour de fête," p. 49 (entry 152).

33.   Jean-Pierre Escande, "Jour de fête," p. 18 (entry 18). My translation.

34.   In an anonymous article, "Voyage à Tativille," p. 19 (entry 157), Tati is quoted as saying that the film cost 17 million D'AF [ancien francs] 1947 and returned 80 million.

35.   Tati in Cauliez, Tati, p. 9 (entry 192). My translation.

36.   Jacques Deheure, "Les Vacances de Monsieur Hulot," p. 2 (entry 35).

37.   Moritz, Current Biography, p. 45 (entry 146).

38.   The NBC special took place in November 1954, since a review of it appeared at that time in the New York Times. Unfortunately, inquiries at NBC reveal that the kinescope of that special has been destroyed.

39.   Jacques Tati, "Jacques Tati reconte son nouveau film Mon oncle," p. 6 (entry 126).

40.   "Voyage à Tativille," p. 19 (entry 157).

41.   Cauliez, Tati, p. 12 (entry 192).

42. Cauliez is the only one to discuss this (pp. 12-13), but he does not specify the precise date of the film's rerelease (entry 192).

43. Cauliez is the only one to discuss this (p. 13), but he does not specify dates (entry 192).

44. Tati in Cauliez, Tati, p. 13 (entry 192). My translation.

45. "Tati and Rohauer Buy Educational Films, 1,000 Shorties, 60 Sennetts" (entry 155).

46. Mentioned in Brent Maddock, The Films of Jacques Tati, p. 24 (entry 312) and in Danièle Heymann and Michel Delain, "Tati: Méfiez-vous des comiques anoblis!" pp. 21-23 (entry 331).

47. Jacques Tati in "Tati," p. 8 (entry 188).

48. Jacques Tati in Jonathan Rosenbaum, "Tati's Democracy," p. 40, (entry 263).

49. "Voyage à Tativille," p. 16 (entry 157).

50. Jean-André Fieschi, "Le Carrefour Tati," p. 24 (entry 194).

51. Thomas Lenoir, "Tati et le temps des loisirs," p. 31 (entry 177).

52. Jonathan Rosenbaum, "Paris Journal," p. 2 (entry 225).

53. Andreas Freund, "Jacques Tati and His Movies Return after Enforced Vacation," p. 14 (entry 309).

54. Jean De Baroncelli, "Playtime de Jacques Tati" (entry 173).

55. Gilliatt, Tati, p. 10 (entry 292).

56. See Pie Dufour, "Jacques Tati, Noted French Comic Comes for Festival" (entry 235) and Don Safran, "Tati Debuts Festival" (entry 243).

57. Mosk, "Parade" (entry 275).

58. Michel Delain, "Tati à l'encan," p. 52 (entry 272).

59. Pierre Montaigne, "Tati s'en va-t-en guerre" (entry 293).

60. Maddock, The Films of Jacques Tati, p. 154 (entry 312).

61. Will Tusher, "Jacques Tati to Make First Hollywood Film," p. 1 (entry 287).

62. Ron Pennington, "Confusion about Confusion," p. 1 (entry 286).

63. Freund, "Tati Returns," p. 14 (entry 309).

64. Maurice Fabre, "Après l'échec de Playtime, le triomphe du festival Tati" (entry 306).

II. Critical Survey

> Great filmmakers . . . are through-
> out their careers, compiling a sin-
> gle work. A new film is simply the
> next chapter.[1]
>
> --Vincent Canby

In the history of cinema, there are those filmmakers whose work
might be thought of as encyclopedic--with each film exploring a new
issue or problem. Charles Chaplin can be viewed in such epic terms,
with Modern Times (1936) probing the subjects of technology and labor,
The Great Dictator (1940), the topics of war and fascism, and The Gold
Rush (1925), the twin issues of materialism and greed.

There are other artists, however, of equal stature whose work is
more comparable to variations on a theme. Orson Welles appears to
have worked in this manner. Though his sources range from Shakespeare
to Kafka, and his settings from the middle ages to the present, his
concern is perennially the politics of power--be it crystallized
through the persona of Macbeth, Othello, Hank Quinlan, or Charles
Foster Kane.

Jacques Tati is a filmmaker of this second type. For his work,
in its totality, presents a clear, considered, and profound explora-
tion of a select number of themes. To use Canby's metaphor, each
film is essentially a new chapter of an ongoing text. Thus, it is
not surprising to find in his first feature, Jour de fête, traces of
all the concerns that will animate his subsequent work: a suspicion
of modern technology, a distress with twentieth-century alienation,
a regret of the degradation of leisure, a hostility toward the commercial film industry. Similarly, it seems fitting that later films
constantly propel one back to the earlier work. Thus Playtime's final
scene of the traffic jam/carousel sparks associations with the central
image of Jour de fête--the old village merry-go-round.

Yet in Tati's work, the resurfacing of issues is never mere

repetition. Each time a theme reappears, it is subtly reworked and
seen from a new perspective. Given this rigorous thematic unity, it
is profitable to construct an overview of Tati's films, tracing the
evolution of concerns across his oeuvre.

The Shadow of the Assembly Line

> Dividing and subdividing operations,
> keeping the work in motion—those
> are the keynotes of production.[2]
> —Henry Ford

Because Tati's films are essentially works of comic satire, they
address profoundly serious issues within contemporary society. It is,
therefore, necessary to discuss their cultural commentary in order to
apprehend their humor.

The theme that is most often identified with Tati is the critique
of modern technology and industrial decor. Brent Maddock, for example, speaks of Tati's films as centering on "the common reality of
automobiles, highways, skyscrapers and garbage disposals."[3] Gerald
Mast cites the "foes" in Tati's films as "modernity, inhuman efficiency [and] deadening routine."[4] Armand Cauliez describes Tati as "on
the warpath" against modern-age values, attacking the contemporary
myths of "organization, mechanization, comfort and speed."[5] But simply to identify this theme in broad monolithic terms is not sufficient.
For Tati is satirizing specific aspects of twentieth-century culture.
It is, in fact, the particularity of his critique that spares it from
being vague and cliché.

In a very insightful study of Buster Keaton's The General (1926),
Noël Carroll has discussed the importance of the issue of industrialization and assembly-line production for an understanding of Keaton's
comic style.[6] The same perspective might be brought to bear on the
work of Jacques Tati, for in his comic vignettes of contemporary life,
the assembly line is a lead character. In several of Tati's films,
it appears quite literally on screen. In others, however, it is a
kind of off-screen presence which casts a looming shadow on stage.

The assembly line makes its initial appearance in Tati's short
film, L'École des facteurs, which was eventually extended into Jour
de fête. The latter concerns a French village postman, François
(Tati) who sees a documentary film on the American postal system and
is convinced by his fellow townspeople to "modernize" his mail delivery. The documentary emphasizes the assembly-line mechanization of
the American postal process: airplanes drop mail in remote places;
conveyor belts sort packages; and letters are mechanically stamped.
Mail delivery is parceled out into a series of discrete tasks, and
machines are utilized whenever possible in place of human beings.
The watchwords of this process are speed and efficiency.

Throughout the mock-documentary, it is emphasized that this system is quintessentially American and that, in a gesture of missionary

zeal, the Yankees will soon make their expertise available to their
backward European allies.

In contrast to the American system, François's rural, Gallic
postal mode is casual, sporadic, and lackadaisical. He enacts all
phases of the process himself, often interrupting his duties to chat
with a townsman or help a farmer in the field. His less than machine-
like precision regularly leads to comic errors and mishaps.

When François attempts to apply the assembly-line logic to his
primitive postal operations, all hell breaks loose. To accelerate
the process, he stamps envelopes while his bicycle is hitched to the
back of a moving truck. To speed delivery, he begins depositing his
mail in unlikely, but convenient places--on the prongs of a hoe or
under a horse's tail. Eventually, an old village woman urges François
to return to his quaint, preindustrial ways. "News is bad enough,"
she tells him. "We don't need to get it in such a hurry."

The next direct appearance of the assembly line in Tati's films
comes with Mon oncle. Here, the French are no longer portrayed as in-
adequate imitators of American industrial production. The assembly
line has already made inroads into the French environment.

In Mon oncle, Tati plays M. Hulot--a whimsical and unemployed mis-
fit who lives in the old part of Paris. At one point in the film,
Hulot's brother-in-law, M. Arpel, the owner of a plastics factory,
secures for him a position "on the line." Hulot, however, is so bored
with his monotonous job that he falls asleep at work, and the plastic
tubing, whose production he oversees, emerges from the machine with
inexplicable bulges and bubbles. The entire assembly-line process is
then interrupted as Hulot and his fellow workers attempt to sneak the
unsightly tubing out of the plant.

The final appearance of the assembly line as a literal presence
in Tati's films comes in Trafic, where the opening credit-sequence
presents documentary material of automobile production. Typically,
however, even in dealing with this authentic footage, Tati depicts
the process running wild. For if we observe the production line
closely, we notice a dented car door being produced. Though this is
the only assembly-line image seen in the film, factory production remains in the background throughout, since the narrative of Trafic concerns the manufacture of cars.

Given the presence of the assembly line in Tati's films, what
precisely is his point of view on the issue of mechanization? Since
Tati's broad subject is a critique of contemporary culture, the assembly line clearly figures into this discourse as a major and unavoid-
able symbol of industrialization. When Tati depicts the assembly line
within the narrative of his films, what he primarily satirizes is its
perverse inefficiency--its propensity to run hopelessly amok.
François's mechanized postal round in Jour de fête is high-speed

chaos; Hulot's episode on the assembly line in Mon oncle results in disaster; even the Renault production plant in Trafic goes out of control. This ironic perspective on technology is the legacy of Charlie Chaplin's Modern Times--where the Tramp sabotages the assembly line and utimately becomes its victim.

Tati, however, has other, more personal, complaints about the assembly line which relate to his position as a film director. For in addition to having transformed industrial production, the assembly line has also influenced the making of film art. It is, of course, no secret that the Hollywood studio is an arts-oriented factory, modeled on the assembly line. Each job in the creation of a film (be it cinematography, editing, costuming, or lighting) is parceled out to a specialized worker, and the finished product is then marketed as a salable commodity, like a refrigerator or an automobile.

As an independent film director, Tati has always been opposed to this assembly-line filmmaking process. He has raised the money for his films himself, written his own scripts, and supervised the camera work, editing, and sound mixing for all his productions. Thus his modus operandi is more like a nineteenth-century craftsperson (who participates in the entire process of fashioning an object) than it is like a twentieth-century worker. "I am an artisan," he has said. "And if I defend it, it is because I am alarmed by the manner in which the cinema has recently been functioning."[7]

From this perspective, the narratives of several Tati films take on an added dimension. Jour de fête's satirization of the postal documentary from the United States not only opposes the Marshall Plan ethic but also the imposition of American cinema (that quintessential assembly-line film product) on the war-decimated French film industry. Similarly, the narrative of Trafic takes on new meaning, for Hulot is cast there as a commercial artist, hopelessly unsuited to the task of designing automobiles. Thus, his position parallels that of Tati, an artist caught in the commercial industry of film. Tati has frequently utilized an automotive metaphor to describe the problematics of filmmaking. On one occasion, he criticized money-minded producers who force directors to put together films in the manner of a car--combining best-selling novels, famous scenarios, box-office stars--to produce a surefire cinema success. As Tati phrased it:

> That is valuable for [producing a car]--in taking the
> best cushioning device, the best gear box, the best
> motor, one can fit them together and be assured that
> it will work. But the cinema--it is not at all the
> same thing.[8]

Aside from faulting the assembly line for its takeover of commercial film production, Tati also articulates more general complaints about its influence on modern culture. Essentially, his criticism focuses on two basic issues: the malign effect of the assembly line

on the realm of human behavior, and its imprint on the objects and
architecture inhabiting our machine-age landscape.

Behavior: The Phantom of Liberty

Even in films in which the assembly line does not make a direct
appearance, one senses its presence in the realm of human behavior.
One is again reminded of <u>Modern Times</u>--particularly of the sequence
in which Charlie continues to perform his bolt-tightening task even
when he is off the line. It is this mark of the machine on human
functioning that fascinates Tati. And one sees this theme reiterated
over the course of his work, each time with a slightly different emphasis.

In general, Tati confronts the influence of the assembly line on
human behavior by observing people at leisure--a time when one would
assume its effect to be less potent and pronounced than when at work.
But clearly this assumption is false. What Tati reveals is that,
ironically, the "free time" society gains through assembly line practice is not really free in any qualitative sense of the word. Rather,
contemporary leisure is spent in a mechanical fashion which mirrors
the very work process that spawned it. As Frankfurt school critics,
Theodor Adorno and Max Horkheimer, have put it:

> [Leisure] experiences are inevitably after-images of
> the work process itself . . . whatever happens at work,
> in the factory, or in the office, can only be escaped
> from by approximation to it in one's leisure time.[9]

The film in which this issue is most clearly rendered is <u>Les
Vacances de Monsieur Hulot</u>. Though the film portrays a French seaside
resort and depicts an ostensible vacation, the world of the Hotel de
la Plage seems more like that of the office or factory. Thus, the
very same time schedules and routines obtain at the Hotel de la Plage
as do in the workaday world. The meal bell rings at regular intervals
and everyone obediently assembles; conversations take the form of
verbal ready-mades; every day ends in a requisite manner, with an
evening of cardplaying in the hotel parlor.

Thus, though the work world is never directly represented in the
film, it seems to hover around the frame like an unspeakable off-
screen presence. Although the vacationers are away from the work
place, the machine-age sensibility attaches itself to their very behavior. They spend their supposedly liberating vacation in repeti-
tive, mechanical leisure-time "tasks" and ultimately "treat their
holiday like a job."[10] If the Hotel de la Plage is not the workaday
world itself, it is surely its negative image.

The aura of the assembly line is even more pronounced in <u>Playtime</u>.
Again the film concerns people at leisure--this time some Americans
abroad. But Tati takes great pains to demonstrate the very mechanization of their vacation. The travelers arrive on a guided tour that

whisks them passively through their precious vacation days like objects on an assembly-line belt. At stop number one, they see the Eiffel Tower and at stop number two, a Parisian restaurant. Significantly, one of their main tourist activities is a visit to a trade exposition where they sightsee production-line consumer artifacts.

By the time of Trafic, Tati's point of view on the issue has changed a bit. Rather than observe human behavior on vacation, he focuses on the leisure industry itself. Thus, M. Hulot is cast as a designer for the Altra automobile company, a business that produces "recreational" vehicles. Tati thereby satirizes the "camping car," with its inflatable beds, its color television, its steak-grill fender, and its hot and cold running water. It is a veritable leisure-time machine--a product designed for people more comfortable on the assembly line than off.

In Mon oncle, Tati views leisure within the context of the modern home. Here he mocks the equalization of factory and household; for the same kinds of machines that populate M. Arpel's plastics plant are found in his home. Thus Mme. Arpel uses a mechanical device to sterilize her son's dinner plate or to defumigate his body in lieu of a conventional bath. Tati seems to be questioning the status of such a home as a refuge from the work place, since its harsh domestic atmosphere makes it a virtual factory-surrogate. Clearly any leisure time the Arpels spend there cannot help but be compromised.

Tati's concern with the relation of work and leisure seems tied to an earlier film in French history--À nous la liberté (1931) by René Clair. For Clair, like Tati, equates assembly-line work with intolerable repression, but posits a utopian future when machines will accomplish all human labor. Thus he ends À nous la liberté with a blissful vision of workers at leisure, while machines produce goods without their participation. Tati sees no such pot of gold at the end of the technological rainbow. Though machines can release us from human labor, they can also leave their imprint upon our lives. Hence leisure may be spent in mechanical fashion or filled with industrial products that leave us spiritually devoid. Thus, Tati perceives that contemporary people at leisure are not always truly liberated. Rather than live their free hours, they often "consume" them--in a desperate effort to kill and fill time.

Central to Tati's view of contemporary leisure is a concern with boredom--a feature recognized early on by the critic Théodore Louis, who called him "un peinture d'ennui."[11] But as a satirist, Tati refuses the portrayal of boredom as heavy existential angst, or philosophic "nauseau"--but rather depicts it as a brand of comic distraction. Thus his characters wander about with blank, hypnotic stares-- like victims of catatonia or autism. Trivial events are ludicrously protracted into major occasions, as a sense of false suspense informs someone's walk across a room, or the opening of a briefcase. Events proceed in antidramatic fashion and tend to sag like Hulot's infamous taffy, or peter out like the rebound of his wayward Ping-Pong ball.

Tati's world, thus, has a hollow, empty ring to it--like a perfect laboratory vacuum. Hence the comic aspect of certain grossly exaggerated sounds, whose echo seems to emphasize the vacancy of the surrounding world. If this void is comic, it is also deadly and deadening. And part of Tati's humor is, curiously, bound up with a perception of necrophilia subtending our culture. Thus, in part, Tati's comedy is one of morbidity--the humor of animated corpses, of the danse macabre.

Objects and Architecture: Commodity Fetishism and Hi-Tech Decor

But it is not just assembly-line procedures that have come to dominate human behavior: industrial products have also gained influence over our lives. Thus, throughout his films, Tati satirizes the contemporary environment with its mechanical artifacts and hi-tech decor.

In the realm of objects, his favorite comic targets are so-called labor-saving devices, for which the Arpel home is a paradigmatic site. Among other things, Mme. Arpel owns a hamburger flipper and an electric-eye garage door. In Playtime, Tati's satire of objects focuses largely on the trade exposition where he mocks the carpet sweeper with headlights and the temperamental intercom. In Trafic, his main comic subject is the camping car with its myriad ludicrous gadgets.

In general, Tati's comedy locates several problems with such mechanical devices. First, they frequently break down and leave their owners in unspeakable predicaments. In Mon oncle, the Arpels get trapped in their garage when the family dog mistakenly triggers the electric eye; and in Trafic an Altra employee is surprised when gas comes out of the camping car's sink faucet. Furthermore, Tati is upset with the passivity these machines engender in people and cites this issue quite often in interviews:

> Look, cars get bigger and bigger with so many gadgets there is nothing left for the driver to do. He can go to sleep, the car will drive itself . . . Machines not only do the work, they also do the thinking.[12]

For Tati, yet another danger lurks in the omnipresence of these industrial-age devices and the possibility that human beings themselves will become mechanized. Throughout his films, one encounters robot men who behave more like automata than human beings. The most extreme case is the man in Playtime who waits with Hulot for his appointment with M. Giffard. Every gesture he makes is linear and brittle, as he plays obsessively with his nasal sprays, attaché case locks, and retractable pencils. In this brand of comedy, one is reminded of Henri Bergson's essay "Laughter," (1900) which posits humor as arising from the perception of "something mechanical encrusted on the living."[13]

Finally, Tati sees in consumer goods a modern-day form of the
fetish. For in the Arpel home or the trade exposition, objects function not at the level of real use but as quasi-magical icons, invested
with excessive reverence. What else would explain the Arpels' delir-
ium over an automatic garage door in Mon oncle, or the two tourists'
orgasmic response to a lamp in Playtime?

But Tati's comedy goes beyond a broad satirization of contemporary
objects and includes a humorous investigation of the very substances
of our hi-tech decor. It is significant that in Mon oncle, M. Arpel
runs a plastics factory, since that material has become synonymous
with our industrial age. Many gags in Mon oncle revolve around the
synthetic nature of that substance. In one scene, M. Hulot is alone
in the Arpel kitchen, poking around. By mistake, he drops a pitcher,
which he fully expects will shatter but instead finds bouncing back
at him. When he drops a cup, expecting that it too will be resilient,
it smashes into innumerable pieces.

But it is not just the alien, unpredictable nature of the material
that Tati views as comic but also its hopeless sterility. Thus, he
presents a vision of the Arpel home as a suburban Wasteland. Their
stone and cactus garden is a virtual desert. And their mechanical
fish-shaped fountain (which manages only to retch or regurgitate pol-
luted water) seems an ironic substitute for the fertile Fisher-King.
Clearly, chez-Arpel, industrial necrophilia reigns supreme.

In Playtime, the satirization of the sterile contemporary world
is even more directly associated with plastic. Dazed Parisians in Le
Drugstore unwrap food from Saran Wrap and try to discern what they are
eating. A disoriented M. Hulot tries to get some traction on a slick
plastic floor and ends up executing a split. Moreover, the theme of
aridity (introduced in Mon oncle) is articulated in Playtime through
a contrast of real and plastic flowers. The fresh flowers of the
traditional Parisian street seller are thereby opposed to the snythe-
tic flowers on the tourists' hats and on the walls of a chic restaurant. Even the restaurant's name (The Royal Garden) is a wry misnomer,
since it is a Wasteland like the Arpel yard.

By the time of Playtime, however, the contemporary landscape has
progressed from the era of plastic to the age of steel and glass.
Thus, Tati continually deploys gags based on people's problems navigating in a glass-filled architectural world. Most of these comic
bits occur in the early part of the film when M. Hulot scurries
through a modern high-rise building in search of the elusive M.
Giffard. At one point, when the two men are in fairly close proxim-
ity, M. Hulot catches sight of Giffard's reflection in the glass wall
and mistakes it for the man himself. In the comic chase which follows,
Hulot pursues the phantom reflection in the opposite direction of the
real Giffard. Later in the film, when Giffard spots Hulot outside
the building, he is in such a hurry to greet him that he forgets the
presence of a transparent glass wall and walks into it, injuring his

nose. In a sequence that was cut out of most American release prints, Tati also mocks the lack of privacy allowed by glass. Hulot is seen in one shot standing outside of an apartment building at night, watching all the activities within like the viewer of a proverbial fishbowl.

In these sequences, one gets the sense of human beings as hopelessly vulnerable and stunned by their contemporary surroundings. And it is from their basic inadequacy and confusion in these circumstances that the humor ultimately arises. Tati views people from an almost "evolutionary" perspective--at a particular developmental stage of their species, not yet adapted to the new requirements of the world. Like a dramatic shift in climate or vegetation, these technological changes have descended upon the human environment. And Tati catches people at the comic moment when they wait for adaptation or pray for random mutation. As the writer Antoine de Saint-Exupery put it in Terre des hommes:

> Everything has changed so rapidly around us; human
> relations, conditions of work, customs . . . Every
> step in our progress has driven us a little further
> from our acquired habits and we are in truth pioneers
> who have not yet established the foundations of our
> new country.[14]

It is this stance that accounts for the note of optimism some find in Tati's films.[15] For he assumes that human adaptation is possible and will eventually take place. As Tati has said, it was his purpose in Playtime to show "that . . . we will always escape danger, [that we] will always know how to adapt this decor to [our] behavior."[16]

Tati believes that such adaptation is probable because he does not see technology as a totally alien force. Rather, he recognizes that it has been fashioned by human beings in their own image. As Werner Heisenberg has noted:

> The statement that in our time man confronts only
> himself is valid in the age of technology. In earlier
> epochs man saw himself opposite nature. Nature . . .
> was a realm existing according to its own laws and
> into it man somehow had to fit himself. We on the
> other hand live in a world so completely transformed
> by man that whether we are using the machines of our
> daily life, taking food prepared by machines or
> striding through landscapes transformed by man, we
> invariably encounter structures created by man, so
> that in a sense we always meet ourselves.[17]

It is the perception of this apparent paradox that informs Tati's critique and saves it from a facile opposition of Nature and Technology.

In addition to satirizing contemporary mechanical objects and hi-tech construction materials, Tati also lampoons modern architecture and design in his films. (The character of M. Hulot is, in fact, based on an architect that Tati once knew.)[18] Tati's critique begins with the suburban home of M. and Mme. Arpel in Mon oncle, but it is the office building in Playtime that is the central figure of this concern. The glass walls, which look out upon the Parisian street, deny any sense of shelter and make one feel adrift in the midst of traffic. The elevators, which perversely blend into the walls, are easily mistaken for mere corners of the hall. The long corridors, with flooring that echoes every footstep, make it difficult to sense when a person is approaching. The endless, uniform office cubicles isolate people and turn the work place into a maze. Again, human behavior is affected: in buildings with rigorously geometric floor plans, people tend to walk in military straight lines. Clearly, most of the gags in the early section of Playtime are based on the exploitation of such architectural problems: M. Hulot's pursuit of Giffard through the labyrinthian cubicles, his attempt to determine when the latter is approaching down the hall, his entrapment in the "hidden" self-service elevator.

The Arpel garden in Mon oncle is another case in point, where rigid design promotes constrained behavior. Because of the layout of flagstones in the garden, it is only possible for people to approach the house by one predetermined path. Several gags occur in the film which are based on this architectural situation. At one point in the garden party, guests are seen walking in the yard single file, like a group of obedient schoolchildren on a class trip. Another gag occurs when, on this S-shaped path, Mme. Arpel tries to greet an incoming guest. Because the shape of the path sends the two women in opposite directions, their outstretched arms blatantly miss each other.

Furniture in Tati's films is subject to a similar critique. The chairs in the Arpel house position the backside dangerously close to the ground, and Hulot must turn the sofa on its side in order to sleep comfortably. In Playtime, office seat cushions emit an unpleasant rush of air, and restaurant chairs leave metallic "brands" on people's backs.

Tati enjoys mocking women's fashions as well, which he sees as unsuitable for bodily comfort. In Jour de fête, he satirizes the pretentious festival get-up of the cafe owner's wife, and in Playtime, he populates Paris with women in straight-skirted black dresses and spike-heeled shoes.

Tati also mocks the uniformity of design in an era of assembly-line production. In Les Vacances, two women are upset to find they are wearing identical tennis outfits. In Playtime, the issue of conformity is articulated on a grander scale. When the American tourists arrive at Orly and see a vast parking lot and a skyline of glass and steel buildings, one asks bewilderedly if the guide is sure this is Paris, France. Later Tati derives much humor from showing us a travel agent's office with posters for London and Honolulu that depict the very same high-rise building. Again this uniformity produces human disorientation. We are all accustomed to jokes about suburbanites who walk into the wrong tract house; but are we prepared for jokes about people walking into the wrong country?

In opposition to this vision of an alienated contemporary society, Tati always manages to introduce into his films the suggestion of an earlier, more idyllic world. Thus, he constantly posits a dialectic of the old and the new--with the figure of M. Hulot strongly identified with the past. Although elements of the old are found in all of Tati's works, it is in Jour de fête that this pole of the continuum is explored in full and in isolation, for the world of Jour de fête is French rural life at its most traditional--with bicycles, animals, and women in aproned long skirts. As opposed to the drugstores or department stores of Playtime, there are village cafés and family-run shops. Instead of the mechanized leisure of Trafic, there is the simple annual fair with its wooden merry-go-round horses and its naive carnival games.

Rather than depict one pole of the continuum exclusively, most of Tati's later films establish a tension between them. In Mon oncle, we have the old quarter of town in which M. Hulot resides contrasted to the Arpels' modern development. In Playtime, small touches of old Paris remain in the flower seller on the street or in the reflection of historic monuments on the glass high-rise doors. In Trafic, there are intimations of a simpler life in the rural Dutch village to which Hulot hikes for gas and in the car mechanic's shack. Whereas Jour de fête represents the pole of old-fashioned simplicity in Tati's early work, Parade is its manifestation in later years. For as Jour de fête portrays the quaint village festival, so Parade presents the traditional circus world.

There is clearly a strong pull toward the past in Tati's films, and a retrospective view informs certain interview statements as well. In a Cue article of November 1958, for example, Tati noted with some dismay:

> The corner grocer is now a supermarket with a million
> shelves and a thousand cash registers. In your subway
> there is no conductor--the doors open themselves, the
> stations are announced by records, and a machine makes
> your change. . . . Is this progress?[19]

This stance has, on occasion, spawned some criticism of Tati. René Guyonnet, for example, wrote in 1958 that Mon oncle evinced a "doltish nostalgia" and a desire for the "good old days."[20] Tati has always denied these charges and claimed that "Hulot is not a reactionary."[21] Furthermore, he has explained that it is not change, per se, that he opposes but the frenetic rate of change typical of the last few decades.[22]

Within the films themselves, it is clear that Hulot never simply retreats from the modern world--the reductio ad absurdum of the nostalgic position. Rather, he reluctantly participates in contemporary society and frequently catalyzes some sort of change. On certain occasions, he openly infiltrates the enemy lines and launches a direct assault. In Les Vacances, Hulot consistently disrupts the world of the Hotel de La Plage with his unconventional tennis game, his loud jazz records, his noisy Ping-Pong ball, and ultimately his fireworks blitzkrieg on the sleeping guests. At other times, he acts more like teacher than aggressor. In Mon oncle, for instance, he succeeds, by example, in humanizing the relationship between M. Arpel and his son. On yet other occasions, Hulot leads a virtual palace revolution. In Playtime, he encourages the Royal Garden guests to destroy the restaurant's sterile decor and set up an alternate bistro space in the rear. Thus, Hulot sees no need to retreat to the past, but rather to bring his traditional values to present contexts.

Often, in so doing, he creates comical situations because of the discrepancy between his quaint behavior and modern ways. In Playtime, he appears ludicrous when he smells his plastic-wrapped sandwich and seems foolish when he responds politely to a salesman's rude tirade against him. Thus, Hulot makes us aware of certain "eccentricities" in our present-day culture that might otherwise go unnoticed.

In this respect, Hulot serves a truly Bergsonian function. For his anachronistic presence in the contemporary world frequently underscores the kind of "mechanical inelasticity" that Bergson suspected of modern societies. The laughter that Hulot inspires, then, can be seen as a kind of "cure" for these cultural ills. For, as Bergson stated, laughter is above all a "social gesture"--and a "corrective," --by which "society avenges the liberties taken with it."[23]

COMIC PERSPECTIVES: WAYS OF SEEING

In addition to seeing laughter as a social corrective, Tati sees it as a personal salvation--a solution to alienation in the modern world. In this respect, he is, essentially, an idealist and a romantic, who valorizes the triumph of the imagination. Rather than espouse any reform of the external world, he advocates a change in individual consciousness as a means of coping with the inhospitable modern environment. Essentially, Tati's films instruct the viewer in two modes of humorous perception: what might be called metaphoric and comic vision. Tati implies that if these visual stances are adopted, the world can be humanized and perhaps enjoyed.

Metaphoric Vision

By metaphoric vision is meant the ability to see things in a figurative fashion, to "transform" one thing into another. As we shall see throughout Tati's career, many gags in his films require the spectator to engage in this process. In Les Vacances, for example, to understand the humor of the sequence in which the old sea captain spies Hulot's collapsing boat through his binoculars, it is crucial that the audience realize that the sinking vessel resembles the jaws of a huge shark. Similarly, in Mon oncle, it is necessary that the audience perceive the two circular windows of the Arpel house as a pair of peering eyes in order to find them comic. Again in Trafic, both the audience and Hulot's colleague, Maria, must see a white fur coat as a dead dog in order to appreciate the humor of a sequence in Holland.

But it is in Playtime that this mode of metaphorical vision is fully explored and made the basis of much of the comedy. Thus, one gag is based on the audience seeing highway lights as bluebells, and another on their viewing a neon sign as a halo. At one point, a sponge must be seen to resemble a piece of Swiss cheese, and at another, a kitchen pass-through must be seen as a Napoleonic hat. This kind of metaphoric vision is solicited from the very first shot of the film in which nuns' hats are made to resemble flapping seagulls. Even the entire first sequence at Orly is based on the spectator's mistaking the airport for a hospital. But the most sophisticated comic sequence of this type occurs at the very end of Playtime when Tati transforms a Parisian street into a fairgrounds, and a traffic jam into a carousel.

Once more it might be said that Tati's emphasis on metaphorical vision is comparable to Chaplin, who endowed the Tramp with a "transformational" kind of imagination. In The Pawnshop (1916), for example, Charlie treats a feather duster like a bird and keeps it in a cage. And when he takes apart an alarm clock, he treats its case like a can of tuna and its innards like a band of scurrying cockroaches. Similarly, in The Gold Rush (1925), Chaplin treats a shoe like a gourmet dish--filleting its sole and eating its laces like spaghetti.

Whereas in Chaplin's films it is only the Tramp who has the capacity for such "special" vision, in Tati's films that power is not reserved for a comic virtuoso but encouraged in the spectator's own perception. It is Tati's implicit hope that upon leaving the theater the viewer will utilize such a visual point of view to cope with an alien world.

Comic Vision

But Tati also bases much of the humor in his films on yet another visual stance--one that might be called comic vision. Although many gags in Tati's films are based on the eccentricities of Hulot's behavior (his penchant for opening the hotel lobby door, his peculiar table manners), an equal number are based not on an overtly humorous event but on a normal occurrence as viewed from a comic perspective. This is most apparent in Les Vacances, where many gags are dependent on comic vision as rendered through the camera's visual point of view. Thus, some of the gags in the film are based not on a comic incident but on the visual framing of an everyday event. In one scene in the film, the young woman, Martine, and her aunt are sitting in their second-floor dining room. Through a window we see a beach ball intermittently float up and down. That the ball is tossed is not inherently comic. What makes it humorous is that its framing leaves the launcher out of sight.

Other gags in the film result from the angle of vision from which an event is viewed. Once more, in deriving comedy from a particular visual/spatial stance, Tati is invoking a form of humor based not so much on what is happening but on how it is seen. In one particular sequence, Hulot walks around a beach shack in which Martine is changing her clothes and discovers an American businessman standing at the side of the shack with a camera. Hulot's angle of vision is such that the beach shack hides from his view a group of the American's friends who are posing for a snapshot. Thinking the American a Peeping Tom, Hulot kicks him in the rear. There is, clearly, nothing inherently funny about a man taking a photograph while on vacation. But there is something comic about an angle of vision that makes an innocent man resemble a degenerate voyeur.

Although in Les Vacances, Tati renders his comic vision through the framing and angling of the camera lens, the kind of comedy he presents is meant to be analogous to the sort of humor we can apprehend in the "real" world through our own eyes. For this reason critics have often spoken of Tati's style as involving a realistic "comedy of observation." Roy Armes, for example, has written:

> The basis of Tati's music-hall act and hence of all
> his art is observation. He always has a notebook
> with him in which he can jot down his observation
> of human foibles and quirks of behavior.[24]

But though critics have remarked on this notion of observation, they have not noticed its particularly visual bias. More than simply portraying events that might take place in the everyday world, Tati is also advocating a certain methodology of vision, a particular mode of observation. Because they have not examined this issue, critics have also failed to notice the presence of literal "observer-figures" in Tati's films. Often Tati depicts characters in the midst of making a comic observation—an act that he hopes the spectator will learn as well. Thus the observer-figures function both as characters within the narrative and as obvious viewer-surrogates. Some examples will make this strategy clear. As early as Jour de fête, a gag occurs in which a man on a hill sees François at some distance below, riding his bicycle. Suddenly the man notices François gesturing inexplicably, waving his gangling arms in the air. The man is puzzled. What the audience knows (but the observing man does not) is that François is warding off a bee. Thus, though bee attacks are decidedly not comic,

28

they can appear to be when viewed from a particular perspective. Similarly, in Les Vacances, the hotel waiters are perplexed when they peer out a second-story window and see M. Hulot pulled behind a stable by some seemingly invisible force. What the audience knows (but the waiters do not) is that a horse is hidden behind the shed, and its reins are caught on Hulot's boots. Finally, in Playtime, when Hulot is in the office building courtyard, chasing the reflection of M. Giffard, he is observed by a man in an office above to whom the reflection of M. Giffard is not visible. We realize that from the man's perspective, M. Hulot appears to be an ambulatory lunatic.

Tati himself has commented on the possibilities of this type of comic vision, not only in films but in the real world. In an interview with André Bazin and François Truffaut, for example, he related the following relevant anecdote:

> I am going to tell you something that I would have
> wanted to put in a film . . . One day I saw a man who
> wanted to have the oil of his car changed. Since he
> was very rushed, he remained in his car saying:
> "Hurry up! I don't have time; anyway, I have my
> paper to read." . . . This man was very fat, seated
> reading his newspaper. They began to unscrew the
> oil cap under him and then it appeared as though the
> man were seated on the "pot." . . . there are a tre-
> mendous number of things in the world that would be
> passed by without being noticed; it is this genre of
> detail that is irresistible to me. I have wanted to
> stop people, saying "Look!"[25]

Thus for Tati, the comic effect is not solely to be found in the realm of screen comedy; rather, it is available to people in their experience of everyday life. If one has metaphorical and comic vision, one can discover humor in the normal world. Because of this perspective, Tati's art has a didactic dimension--an orientation that links Tati to such ancient comic poets as Aristophanes.[26] In watching Tati's films, one learns a virtual methodology of vision which can then be applied to the external world. In this vein, it is interesting that a critic once remarked how he and some friends laughed at their reflections in a glass door upon exiting a screening of Playtime.[27]

Because of this interest in the comedy of everyday life, Tati has invested the persona of Hulot with a great sense of realism. Rather than make him a burlesque clown, he is more of an average guy, un type. It was clearly out of this need to develop an Everyman comic hero that Tati abandoned the character of François in Jour de fête. Though, as a town mailman, François was situated in a normal context, he was more the buffoon than M. Hulot, more a ridiculous village idiot than a mildly eccentric gentleman. As Tati has said, what he tried to do after Jour de fête was "to give the comic personality more truth."[28]

In this respect, the character of Hulot resembles the comic personae of Buster Keaton or Harold Lloyd. But Tati's conception of Hulot is, in fact, more radical. For though Lloyd and Keaton are superficially realistic, they are nonetheless extraordinarily inventive and agile individuals in the face of adverse circumstances—be it the need to scale a tall building or to operate a locomotive during the Civil War. Tati, however, does not see Hulot as a "brilliant comic." "He's a man," Tati has remarked. "I never give him the chance to be a gag man."[29]

What Tati means by this is that although Hulot is often the source of comic events in the films (drying a beach pole instead of his body in Les Vacances, skidding on an office floor in Playtime), he is generally refused intentionality in the creation of gags. The humor he produces is almost accidental, seemingly untinged by his will. Again Tati's own discussion of the issue is most lucid:

> I'll take the case of a gag that you have seen in Les
> Vacances de Monsieur Hulot. M. Hulot arrives at the
> cemetery. He needs to get his car to start off again,
> looks for a crank in the rear trunk. In looking for
> the crank he throws out a tire. This tire falls on
> the ground and some leaves come to stick on the tube;
> the tire is transformed into a wreath; and the funeral
> director believes M. Hulot has come to bring it. You
> tell me . . . that: "Hulot has not invented any gag."
> That is precisely right.[30]

Tati's point becomes even clearer when he contrasts Hulot's behavior with what he imagines would be that of Chaplin's Tramp. He says:

> In the case of Chaplin . . . he would have made the
> same entrance as Hulot. But seeing that the situa-
> tion is catastrophic (there is a religious service
> going on and his car interrupts this service) find-
> ing himself opening the trunk, with a tire, he would
> have, for the spectator, stuck the leaves on the tire
> himself.[31]

Because he views Hulot as an average fellow, rather than an inspired clown, Tati has become progressively more interested in generalizing the comic effect to other characters. Playtime is the most radical film in this respect since Hulot is seen only intermittently, and it is really the American tourists, the airport personnel, the restaurant workers, and the people of Paris who constitute the comic heroes. As Tati has stated, "I'd eventually like to make a film without a central character, with nothing but the people I observe and pass on the street and prove to them that . . . the comic effect belongs to everyone."[32] For this reason critics like Jonathan Rosenbaum

30

have talked about the "democratic" thrust of Tati's work.[33] Rather
than regarding the comic sense as belonging to an artistic elite,
Tati views it as a basic credential of humanity. As he has stated,
"You won't find another Chaplin or another Keaton . . . now. One has
to look at the people on the streets."[34]

In this respect, Tati's comedy participates in what Freud would
call the comic rather than in classic wit.[35] Whereas, in a Chaplin
film, the viewer functions as a passive audience for Charlie's con-
sciously created "jokes,"--his eating of the shoe, his dance of the
Oceanna Roll--in Tati's films, there is no extraordinary jokester to
observe. Rather, the audience is encouraged to discover comedy in the
situations placed before them, as they might in the "real" world.
Hence, their role is more active and the humorous effect less tied to
a single, precocious comic artist.

Homo Ludens

Although Hulot is clearly a more realistic character than the
comic personae of Chaplin, Langdon, and Keaton, he, nonetheless,
functions within Tati's films as an archetypal figure -- a symbolic
locus for certain values. As mentioned earlier, Hulot is generally
identified with the pretechnological past, an orientation he shares
with certain female characters and children, in Tati's films. In
Les Vacances, Hulot's soul mate is a young woman, Martine, who sympa-
thizes with his impatience at the grim hotel world. In Mon oncle, his
vision is appreciated by his nephew Gérard. In Playtime, Hulot discovers the one imaginative tourist in the American group, a young
woman named Barbara. And in Trafic, he transforms a harsh, Altra "P.
R." lady into a compatriot. Hulot has much the sense about him of a
nineteenth-century French Pierrot clown: his identification with the
spiritual order, his distanced infatuation with women, his affinity
for small children. As one critic has put it, Hulot is a "white moon-
struck clown."[36]

But in addition to these qualities, the figure of Hulot (like
Pierrot) is also strongly identified with the spirit of play--not the
aggressive, slapstick variety practiced by Harlequin, but the more
refined, poetic, and cerebral mode.

That Hulot, as a clown figure, should also be linked to a spirit
of play is not surprising, since parallels have often been made between the comic and ludic stance. James Sully, for example, in An
Essay on Laughter (1902), stated that comedy grew out of the act of
"play-challenge."[37] And Henri Bergson, in "Laughter," noted how the
comic hero seemed a "mere toy in the hands of another who is playing
with him."[38]

But how precisely does the ludic sense evince itself in the character of Hulot? In Les Vacances, we see Hulot counter the rigor mor-
tis of the vacation world with his playful unpredictable tennis style,
his jazz records, and his loud Ping-Pong game. In Playtime, he

31

participates in the destruction of the chic Royal Garden restaurant and its transformation into a bistro where people merrily sing and dance. In Trafic, he helps sabotage the industrial "recreational vehicle," and in so doing, emancipates the Altra staff for an unexpected adventure. But it is in Mon oncle that Hulot's tie to play is strongest, since he liberates his nephew Gérard from the constraints of his antiseptic environment. Thus Hulot allows him to play mischievously with his friends and gives him simple toys (like whistles) rather than the "educational playthings" purchased by his parents.

Although Hulot stands for the spirit of "wholesome" play, Tati situates him in a modern world in which the ludic spirit has gone awry. Instead of a rural merry-go-round, we have an urban traffic-jam carousel; instead of children's games like hide-and-seek, we have Hulot and Giffard's frustrating chase through the architectural labyrinth of the high-rise office building. But this dialectic of pure and distorted play comes out best in Les Vacances. As a final celebration, the Hotel de la Plage has scheduled a masquerade. Although the guests are above this sort of unsophisticated entertainment and do not attend, Hulot, Martine, and the children come in full costume. It is clear, however, that Tati views the guests' abstention from this event ironically. For although unable to attend a true costume ball, they inhabit a modern world that is nothing short of an elaborate social and technological masquerade.

Clearly Tati's concern with the perversion of play is an aspect of his larger critique of contemporary work and leisure. Whereas leisure time is devoid of all ludic spirit--the conduct of daily business seems like nothing so much as a farcical game.

FORMAL STRUCTURES: THE SHAPE OF CONTENT

In The Shape of Content, artist Ben Shahn remarks that it is "impossible to conceive of form as apart from content."[39] This notion of an inextricable bond between structure and meaning is nowhere more apparent than in the work of Jacques Tati. For Tati is not simply a stylistic innovator, pioneering new comic forms. Rather every stylistic strategy contributes to the articulation of a complex thematic statement.

Long-Shot/Long-Take Style

Tati is, of course, best known for his prevalent use of the long-shot/long-take format--a stylistic proclivity tied to the tradition of Jean Renoir. As early as Jour de fête, entire comic sequences are rendered in this manner. In one scene, for example, François enters the village post office. As the camera remains static, he repeatedly disappears from view (into an off-screen dressing room) and then reappears making comic gestures--all in a single long-take shot. Les Vacances contains numerous instances of the long-shot/long-take format. There is the chaotic opening train-platform sequence in which crowds of travelers scurry around the stairwells, looking for the proper departure gate, or the hotel parlor scenes in which groups of guests play cards and listen to the radio. In Mon oncle, there is the long-shot/long-take sequence in which M. Hulot climbs the stairs of his apartment building, or that of the Arpel garden party. And in Trafic, there are the shots of the chaotic Altra factory as Hulot and company depart for the automobile show, or those depicting the mass of activity at the Amsterdam exposition. But the most radical and extensive use of the long-shot/long-take is in Playtime, particularly in the Royal Garden sequence.

But Tati's choice of this mode of shooting is not purely formal: rather the long-shot/long-take style advances certain concepts central to his overall point of view. First, it relates to his quest to bring a sense of realism to his comedy, in order to communicate that the humorous effect belongs to us all. Like the film theorist, André Bazin, he identifies film realism with the long-shot/long-take format --in contradistinction to montage style.[40] Clearly, this position has its theoretical pitfalls, but we can comprehend how Tati might employ the long-shot/long-take mode in the belief that it will open a verit-able "window onto the world."[41]

Beyond this attempt at realism, Tati has other reasons for select-ing this shooting style. For again, like Bazin, he views the format as encouraging more active spectator participation than the alternate montage method. Given the themes of Tati's work, one can see why this notion would appeal to him. While depicting a mechanized, automated world in which the individual is hopelessly passive, he wishes to of-fer the spectator a filmic style that necessitates an active cognitive response, that avoids being a facile recreational vehicle. Again Tati himself is quite lucid on this issue. For in discussing his use of the long-shot/long-take style in Playtime, he has said, "I want[ed] to . . . make people participate a little more, to let them change gears themselves: not to do their work for them."[42]

Finally, Tati's choice of the long-shot/long-take mode can be seen as a rejection of montage editing for its similarity to the assembly-line method. For in the montage style, one can see trans-lated into aesthetic terms the principle of "division and reassembly" which social commentators like Siegfried Giedion have identified with factory practice.[43]

But how precisely might we describe the dynamics of Tati's long-shot/long-take style; and how can it be seen to encourage audience involvement and cognition? To begin with the long-shot itself, Tati's use of this format creates certain cognitive difficulties for the spectator by refusing to emphasize details as one might through the close-up or medium-shot. Rather than presenting gags to the viewer with utmost cognitive clarity, the long-shot structures gags so that they are often difficult to apprehend and subject to the spectator's deciphering.

There are, for example, certain instances in which Tati's use of a long-shot format simply makes it difficult for the spectator to notice a gag which is taking place. In these cases, the spectator's perceptual problems arise from the fact that the scale of objects within the frame is rather small; that the frame is relatively full; and that the shot duration is not long enough to allow an adequate reading of the frame. Often the spectator perceives a glimpse of something comic occurring, but does not appreciate its full implications. The shot is over before the viewer has taken everything in.

Shots of this type occur in many of Tati's films. In Les Vacances, one thinks of a particular evening scene in the hotel parlor when Hulot meets a German camper who is about to depart with her friends for an outdoor cabin. Hulot cavalierly helps her with her backpack, and as he hoists it up onto his shoulders, a stream of water (from a canteen inside) shoots over his head. Because the stream of water is small and transparent, and because there is no close-up of it, it is easy to overlook. Hulot's awkward gesture of hoisting the pack, in fact, deflects our attention from it.

In Playtime, of course, it is easy to miss the joke on the uniformity of modern urban decor if one fails to notice the posters on the wall of the crowded tourist office, which represent various international cities as looking identical. Tati himself best sums up this use of the long-shot. He states:

> The trouble with today's audiences is that they're not
> used to participation, they're used to television which
> makes no demands on the part of the viewer. I do not
> make close-ups of people so the audience must see what
> they see with their own eyes, not what the camera
> tells them.[44]

In many of his films, Tati also forces the spectator to compare items within the long-shot frame in order to get the humor of a particular gag. One thinks of the sequence in Les Vacances in which a waiter in the foreground slices pieces of meat while guests enter the dining room in the background. Unless the viewer compares the two planes of action, the fact that the size of the diner determines the size of the meat being carved will be overlooked. Likewise in Playtime, one is reminded of the shot of tourists on the up and down escalators in the hotel lobby. Unless the viewer compares the entering travelers (with the flowers on their hats drooping) to those departing (with their floral decorations perky and upright), the humor will be missed.

Another way in which Tati utilizes the long-shot/long-take format to create cognitive problems is by deploying multiple gags and events simultaneously within the frame. This technique reaches its culmination in Playtime where the viewer is constantly required to search the frame to get a joke or follow the story line. This style has led critics to liken Tati's mise-en-scène to a "three-ring circus," where spectator attention must shift between coterminus actions. An instance of this phenomenon occurs in the Royal Garden sequence in a shot involving three gags happening at the same time. In the foreground, a humorous pantomime evolves in which a waiter refuses to wait on tables which are not in his territory even though all of his assigned tables are empty. In the midground, a subtle joke is rendered by having waiters (who are serving behind a partition) look as though they were playing the vibes heard on the sound track. Finally, in the background, the louvered kitchen doors reveal the silhouette of a ladder--a sign that the restaurant is in a state of disrepair.

Clearly, Tati thinks of the long-shot/long-take format as offering the spectator a certain degree of freedom. Unlike the modus operandi of the technological devices depicted in his work, he sees his own film as requiring active human participation and cognition. Thus, Tati sees his filmic style as an antidote to the assembly-line mentality which, in the words of sociologists Charles Walker and Robert Guest, requires "surface mental attention as against mental attention in depth."[45]

Though, as critics like Jonathan Rosenbaum have perceptively demonstrated, Tati's long-shot/long-take style does encourage a degree of perceptual freedom, it is important not to simplify the issue. For there are ways in which Tati controls the spectator's attention as well. Thus, in truth, he subtly urges the viewer to notice certain elements within the chaotic frame by underscoring gags through his use of color, camera movement, or sound. At one moment, he may track into an object crucial for the realization of a joke, or color an object in the frame so brightly that it attracts the spectator's glance.[46]

Framing

In addition to the long-shot/long-take format, Tati employs other strategies to challenge the viewer's attention. Among them is his style of visual framing, which often keeps elements of the action offscreen. By framing shots in this particular fashion, Tati forces the spectator to imagine certain events in order to appreciate the gag. Exemplary of this technique is the scene in Les Vacances in which Hulot trips on the stairs to the cottage of Martine's aunt and awkwardly plunges through the house. The camera pans along with him until he passes a statue in the rear garden. As Hulot drifts out of frame, the camera holds on the statue as a vine attached to it unfurls and a crashing sound is heard off-screen. We do not see Hulot fall; we can imagine any details we so desire.

Sound

Tati also employs off-screen sound to stimulate the viewer's intellectual participation. At one point in Les Vacances, the hassled hotel waiters go into the kitchen, but the camera remains on the landing outside. From off-screen, however, we hear the sound of a fight and are encouraged to imagine what is taking place out of view. Correspondingly, in Playtime, it is often an off-screen sound that is the key to a particular joke. Thus, it is the sound of an airplane revving up in the opening shots of the Orly sequence that helps us to establish that the space is not a hospital but an airport, and an off-screen motor sound in the Royal Garden restaurant that signals the repair of the air-conditioning system. Some gags depict the sound source on-screen, but nonetheless challenge us to recognize the nature of the sound. When in a chaotic long-shot, the manager of the Royal Garden is seen dropping something into a glass of wine, it is the fizzing sound that allows us to discern that he is taking an Alka-Seltzer; we thereby get the joke.

Elliptical Gag Structure

Finally, one of Tati's major tools for challenging the spectator's attention is his rather elliptical deployment of gags. In traditional comedies we are accustomed to what is often called a running gag in which elements of a joke occur and reoccur over the course of an entire film. In The Fatal Glass of Beer (1933), each time W. C. Fields opens the door to his Klondike cabin, he utters the exact same phrase and is repeatedly pelted with a blast of snow. Similarly, in Mack Sennett's Love, Loot and Crash (1915), as a mad chase ensues, it repeatedly passes a woman stuck in a barrel.

Tati's variation on the running gag is more complex, for whereas in an ordinary comedy there might be one or two such elliptical comic bits, in a film like Playtime they constitute a major comic structure. A few examples from the film will suffice. Over the course of the Royal Garden sequence, Tati makes fun of the fact that the staff is drinking the wine. The following three shots (deployed elliptically over the duration of a long sequence) can be seen as stages in that gag:

1. The manager walks into the kitchen and looks suspiciously at the wine bottle. He marks the current level of wine.
2. Later, he returns to the kitchen and finds a cluster of waiters around the wine table. He checks the bottle, and we deduce that the wine level is now lower. He blackens the cork with a flame and runs it over the lip of the bottle.
3. Later on, on several occasions, we notice the maitre d' (not the waiters) walk around with a ring around his mouth and realize that he is the culprit.

Another elliptical gag in the Royal Garden sequence concerns the seasoning of a fish entrée and involves the following five stages:

1. A couple orders a fish dish and it is brought to them. A waiter seasons it and leaves it to heat on its chafing dish.
2. Later, another waiter comes by, sees the fish sitting there, and assumes it has not yet been seasoned. He seasons it again as the couple looks on passively.

36

3. A second couple (friends of the seated couple) arrive at the restaurant, and the latter decide to change tables in order to join them.
4. A new couple comes and sits down at the original table by the fish platter.
5. The original waiter now comes by (not noticing that it is a new couple) and flambés the dish and begins to serve it. The new couple are nonplussed and indicate that they have not ordered it. The fish is rolled away.

Play Time

Having catalogued Tati's strategies for challenging the spectator's attention and cognition, it is necessary, however, to understand the implications of his comic style. Why, given the thematic thrust of his work, has he chosen this particular comic mode?

We have already mentioned how Tati's long-shot/long-take style can be read in opposition to the assembly-line subdivision and reconstitution of montage. And we have discussed how his use of that mode stimulates the spectator's involvement, denying the ease of an "automated" film. But there are far more direct ways in which Tati's challenging comic style relates to the content of his work. As discussed earlier, Tati's films often critique the degradation of contemporary leisure, its transformation into a passive, mechanized experience, devoid of the spirit of play. Thus, he has satirized the routinized seaside vacation, the European guided tour, and the recreational vehicle which transplants the suburban home into the midst of the "wild" outdoors. Conversely, he has wistfully recalled such traditional leisure enterprises as the village festival, the bal masqué or the old-fashioned circus.

Within this context, the cognitive challenges posed by Tati's films take on an added dimension and can be seen as constituting virtual leisure-time, audiovisual games, which urge the spectator toward a response of play.[47] Read in this fashion, Tati's films participate in an aspect of comedy long recognized by such theorists as Henri Bergson, who asserted that comedy is "a game that imitates life."[48]

The cognitive problems offered by Tati's films function in two basic ways—to allow us the playful challenges of an audiovisual puzzle and to offer the comic pleasures of deciphering a joke. Critic Raymond Durgnat has commented on the confluence of game and joke structures in another context. He writes:

> An important ingredient in many jokes is the "riddle" atmosphere. Many jokes [and] . . . also many plays on words and ideas, carry the tension of riddles. With their odd or far-fetched associations, they are a little puzzle for the listener, and some of his laughter comes from a pleased relief at solving the riddle, that is "seeing the point."[49]

The work that best demonstrates the notion of film as game is
Playtime, as the title would indicate. Not only do the gags in the
film present the spectator with various cognitive challenges but the
visual format of Tati's shots often bears a remarkable resemblance to
children's paper-and-pencil games. For example, one genre of paper-
and-pencil games is the observation test, which instructs the player
to do something like search a picture for all objects whose names begin with a certain letter. Clearly in *Playtime,* we are never asked
to perform this specific task, but we are required to search the frame
for myriad gags. Another paper-and-pencil game involves the player
searching for figures hidden in an overall design (like cats hidden
in a tree). Again in *Playtime,* we need not perform this specific
task, but we are required to notice hidden crown figures imprinted on
the backs of the Royal Garden diners in order to grasp the humor of
its inhospitable seating decor. Yet another paper-and-pencil game of
wide popularity goes under the title of "Which Two Are Twins?" and requires the player to pick out identical figures in a group of some
eight or ten. Once more, in *Playtime,* we have a comic transposition
of this game, as the viewer is encouraged to notice that all the travel posters on the wall posit endless "twin" cities. Similarly, at
other points in *Playtime* (when the plastic airplane at the Royal
Garden bar melts from overheating or a floor tile sticks to a waiter's
shoe), we are reminded of the paper-and-pencil game, "What's Wrong
with This Picture?"

Because of this formal emphasis on a gamelike mode, Tati's films
can be seen not only to present, on a narrative level, the problem of
passive leisure, but also, in their structure, to inspire in the viewer a playful response. Hence, they act as palliatives for the very
problem they depict. Clearly the relation of structure and signification in Tati's work is extraordinarily tight--the form of his films
addressing the issues of content.

MODERNISM: THE PLEASURES OF THE TEXT

There are several other aspects of Tati's style that warrant examination and make his films relevant not only to the tradition of
film comedy but to the development of film modernism as well.

Signs and Meaning

Current in the discourse of film theory is an interest in analyz-
ing the film image as sign, rather than as naively viewing it as a
transparent analogue of reality. This notion, of course, comes to
cinema largely through the theory of semiology--the science of symbols
and signs. Within this context, Tati's films take on particular relevance to contemporary film theory because his later work (especially
Playtime and *Trafic*) can be seen as elaborate texts on the issue of
signification. French film critic Pierre Baudry, in an essay entitled
"Sur Le Réalisme," was the first to discuss this issue. In speaking
of *Playtime* and *Trafic,* he writes:

> The Tatiesque screen, giving the illusion of being a
> spectacle of the world . . . provides for [the spec-
> tator] a system of indices for deciphering, or better
> than deciphering--for the discovery that everything is
> a sign. What we see is, therefore, not the world but
> its analogic reproduction, each element of which be-
> longs to a signifying chain. One could even assert
> that in this copy of the world, nothing enters which
> does not become an element in the production of the
> sense of the film. All exists to make sense.[50]

It is useful to cite a few specific examples from the films in
order to clarify Baudry's rather complex point. In Playtime, for instance, Tati articulates a message of architectural uniformity, but
often his mode of signifying this concept is quite subtle. At one
point in the film, when the tourist, Barbara, is in her hotel room, a
radio is seen on her window ledge. It is not there, however, simply
as a realistic detail, nor is it there merely to allow Tati an opportunity to burlesque the commercials that it is spewing. Rather it is
there to look like the skyscrapers outside the window and thereby for-
mulate the message of absurd design uniformity, where even radios look
like high-rise buildings. A similar point can be made about the Royal
Garden stage backdrop (which looks like an illuminated skyscraper) and
the office cubicles (which bear a resemblance to steel high-rises).
Rather than being neutral decorative aspects of the frame, they are
elements in the creation of the message of the uniformity of contemporary decor.

Likewise flowers in the film are never there as mere decorative
embellishments or representative aspects of a particular environment.
The artificial flowers on the tourists' hats stand for all that is
lifeless about their culture, as do the plastic flowers in the Royal
"Garden." Dialectically opposed to this are the real flowers of the
old Parisian street seller and the vegetables that we see in the bistro section of the decimated Royal Garden restaurant.

Even characters' garb is carefully coded for meaning. Almost all
the Parisian women in Playtime wear black, or gray, with touches of
white. This simultaneously sums up their conformity and their surface sophistication, as well as their steellike personae. Color in
other of Tati's films is used for a similar process of signification.
The harsh pinks and greens of the Arpels' suburban home in Mon oncle
are meant to contrast with the warm and hospitable terra-cottas of
the old section of town.

Not surprisingly, even the literal signs in the decor of Playtime
have a signifying function. The shape of the Royal Garden's neon
sign, for example, is a backward (mirror-image) question mark, and
tends to bring to the surface a query that forms the subtext of the
sequence, namely, "What are we all doing here?"

A similar point can be made about aspects of the use of glass within the film. Clearly Tati does not make glass so dominant a part of his mise-en-scène simply because it is a common element in contemporary architecture. Rather, through its presence, he articulates a variety of thematic points. On one level, glass seems part of a general comment on the illusory nature of the gifts of progress, and the benefits of modern design and architecture. This notion of glass as illusion is best illustrated in a gag in the Royal Garden sequence. At one point, Hulot breaks the restaurant's glass front door, and thereafter the doorman simply pretends to open a door for the guests, who do not even notice it is not there. What better image could we find for an update of the Emperor's New Clothes?

Obviously in Playtime, glass is not simply used by Tati as a realistic element in the contemporary decor. Rather its prevalence signals that for Tati it stands as an emblem of the contemporary world. Throughout the film, two aspects of glass have been emphasized: its status as quintessential surface of spatial illusion and its quality of fragility. Tati implies that the ideology of any society that opts for glass as its most basic architectural material must share in these qualities of illusion and fragility.

Trafic yields its own examples of this complex mode of meaning, though the significatory process is not as intricate as in Playtime. One theme of Trafic is, of course, the chaos of the modern world; thus Tati portrays society as a topsy-turvy universe which does not know which end is up. Rather than make this statement in any overt fashion, Tati subtly embeds it within the narrative action and mise-en-scène of the film. It is therefore useful to trace the progress of a series of gags which articulate this theme.

    1. In the very first shot of the automobile exposition, we see the auto show sign being put up. A workman on a ladder has put in place the letter O, and his assistant below signals to him to turn it around. The joke here is, of course, that the letter is perfectly round and it makes no difference which end is up.

    2. Later in the film, we see some workmen at the automobile show trying to determine which end of a crate marked in Japanese letters is the top and which the bottom.

    3. In another sequence, when Maria and company finally arrive at the automobile exposition, they find that it is already over. Maria claims that it is impossible since she has written in her date book that the exposition goes on until the ninth. The director of the show, however, informs her that she is mistaken and that it only went through the sixth. Obviously, she has held her date book upside down.

    4. But the tour de force examples in this respect occur at the very end of the film when Hulot is wandering about the deserted auto show. He sees a display car under a sign which says DAF—ostensibly the initials of some automobile company, like VW or BMW. Slowly he gets into the car and tests out the steering wheel, when suddenly the car turns upside down and reveals itself to be only half of a car

shell. Thus, one of the final images of the film is Hulot in the hulk of a car, upside down. While the sign DAF might at first spark associations with the French abbreviation for "anciens francs," it also reminds us of the English words daff and daft, meaning to act or be foolish or insane. Moreover, if the letters are reversed, they spell out fad, another aspect of contemporary madness. Clearly these overtones are not accidental, since this final image is just the culmination of a theme that has been constructed throughout the work: that the values of the world are upside down and hollow; that the world is, ultimately, daffy.

Throughout his film career, Tati has also used concrete sound for signification--eschewing the obvious semantic potential of dialogue in favor of the more elusive possibilities of abstract noise. In general, Tati has utilized highly artificial and exaggerated sound effects for the articulation of his satire on contemporary technology. Thus, he rigorously postsynchronizes his films, frequently using synthetic material as opposed to natural sound. (In Mon oncle, for example, to achieve the sound he wanted for a secretary's footsteps, he synchronized her walk with a bouncing Ping-Pong ball.)[51]

Through his virtuoso sound technique, Tati has extended the borders of film caricature into the realm of the aural burlesque. In Les Vacances, it is the puttering noise of Hulot's old decrepit car that sets it in opposition to the sleek roadsters. In Mon oncle, it is, of course, the gravelly cough of the Arpels' mechanical fish-fountain that signifies the lack of hospitality in their automated home. In Playtime, it is the overwhelming sound of the air-conditioning system in the Royal Garden restaurant, or the unappetizing noise of whipped cream being emitted from an aerosol can, that warns us of the abrasiveness of the contemporary environment. Finally, in Trafic, it is the constant, deafening sound of automobiles that signifies technology's dominance over the human beings it is meant to serve.

Narrative Structure

In addition to a sophisticated mode of signification, Tati's films also display a complex and elusive narrative structure. Most particularly in Les Vacances and Playtime, Tati constructs a highly intricate narrational style that places him firmly in the tradition of such modernist filmmakers as Robert Bresson, Jean-Luc Godard, Alain Robbe-Grillet, or Jean-Marie Straub/Danielle Huillet.

One reason that Tati's narratives suggest this tradition is their radical lack of plot. In discussing Les Vacances, André Bazin described the film's story line as a rather dissociated succession of events, linked by the formula: "And another time, M. Hulot . . ."[52] By the era of Playtime, Tati's narrative construction had become even more tenuous. Thus Tati can summarize the entire plot of the film as follows:

> A group of foreign tourists arrive to visit Paris. In
> landing at Orly they find themselves pretty much in the
> same airport as those which they have left in Munich,
> London or Chicago. They ride in the same buses that
> they had used in Rome or Hamburg; and arrive at a high-
> way bordered by lamps and buildings identical to those
> in their own capital.[53]

Furthermore, Tati's narrative construction, like his gag structure, is characterized by a high degree of ellipsis. He continually
abandons characters for large segments of the drama, only to pick
them up at a later point. Tati himself has commented on this mode of
construction. He said:

> It's always like this in life. Someone arrives, parks
> his car, disappears, you forget, he reappears an hour
> later, etc. It was interesting to base an entire con-
> struction on [this notion]. It is evident that this
> demands an entirely different form of attention on
> the part of the spectator.[54]

Specifically the mode of attention solicited in the spectator might
be likened to that required for a pictorial dot game--where by joining
together a series of points on an otherwise blank page, a coherent
picture is produced.

An example from Les Vacances will make this strategy clear. At
one point in the film, Hulot unwittingly drives his car into the midst
of a cemetery in which a funeral is underway. After the funeral has
ended, Tati cuts to nocturnal shots of the old married hotel guests
walking along the beach and then to Martine playing a record inside
her hotel room. We then hear an off-screen noise and cut to an ex-
terior long-shot of Hulot's car puttering down the road. If we are
very astute, we notice that a man in a top hat (whom we have never
seen before) sits next to him.

Tati has, in a single cut, shifted from Hulot at the funeral during the day to the hotel at night. What has happened to Hulot in the
intervening time is excised from the plot. Our only clue to a connec-
tion between the two events is the man in the top hat. Thus, we sur-
mise that Hulot has been with the party of mourners all day and is
driving back with one of them now.

Similar examples of vague narrative connections abound in Playtime,
most of them having to do with the interrelation of Hulot's activities
with those of the tourist group, the trade exposition salesmen, and
people at the Royal Garden restaurant. For example, in the midst of
a busy airport long-shot in the opening of the film, we must perceive
the figure of M. Hulot dropping his umbrella to realize that he, too,
has just arrived at Orly. We then lose him while the tourist ladies
board their buses. When they later disembark on a Parisian street,

another bus pulls up in the vicinity, and M. Hulot is glimpsed getting off. This elliptical narrative line, whose points of juncture
can be missed at any moment, continues throughout Playtime and culmi-
nates with the barely apprehended sight of M. Hulot wending his way
through the final traffic-jam/carousel.

Reader/Response

Because of their ellipitcal narrative and comic structure, as
well as their complex significatory mode, the films of Tati place
great intellectual demands upon the spectator. As critic Paulette
Pellenq has written, Tati's work is "the opposite of cinema-opium."[55]
In this regard, his films again conform to the modernist aesthetic
which seeks to oppose the alleged "hypnotic spell" of the classical
dramatic film.

Of particular relevance to Tati are certain filmmakers of the
American avant-garde who share with him an interest in the comic/
ludic stance. One thinks of Robert Nelson's Bleu Shut (1970) which
ensnares the viewer in a ludicrous TV guessing game, or of George
Landow's Institutional Quality (1969) which presents the spectator
with an ironic educational "standardized test." Both Tati and these
experimental filmmakers make the viewer acutely aware of a "reader's
response."

Although the Tati spectator is encouraged to participate in a
comic cognitive process, he or she is discouraged from a strong emo-
tive reaction to the film. Like a true Brechtian, Tati avoids character "psychology" and thwarts the viewer's identification with any
screen persona. One has only to compare Chaplin's pathetic Tramp to
Tati's emotionless Hulot to comprehend the aloof nature of Tati's
tone. Although it is a truism that all humor involves an element of
distance, Tati pushes this effect to a radical degree.

Contributing to this sense of distance in Tati's films is their
"monotonous" dramatic structure which levels the story to a uniform
line. There are no real peaks and valleys in Tati's narrative tra-
jectory nor any climaxes or resolutions. Rather, events are characterized by what Jean-André Fieschi has called an "imperturbable
equalization."[56]

Because of these aspects of Tati's style--his distanced stance,
his plotless and elliptical narrative discourse, his complex significatory mode--his work asserts its relevance to the lineage of film
modernism. It is perhaps this realization that informs Cahiers du
cinéma's dual tribute to Tati and Playtime in 1968 and 1979.[57] For
in honoring that film, they pay homage not only to a monument of
screen comedy but to a work whose achievements encapsulate the cinematic developments of a decade. As Jean-André Fieschi has written:

> Innovating . . . with dramaturgy, the frame, the func-
> tion of character, the aural space, the very structure

of the story, Tati merits his place among the most
notable creators of cinematic form today.[58]

THE COMIC TRADITION: A THOUSAND CLOWNS

> Creating laughter is a tradition.
> But little by little, it evolves.[59]
> —Jacques Tati

The Anxiety of Influence

It seems a reflex in the criticism of film comedy to compare one
clown with another—perhaps because comics, more than other types of
artists, are felt to participate in a kinship across historical and
national lines. Such criticism yields provocative insights about the
relationship of various comic personae and places their work in context as part of an ongoing tradition. Ultimately, however, such observations are partial and fragmentary in their critical grasp.
Though a comparative stance can illuminate certain aspects of a filmmaker's work, it clearly leaves others unexamined.

Predictably, the history of critical writing on Tati evinces this
comparative bias. In an early book on the director, Geneviève Agel
relates Jour de fête to the comedy of Mack Sennett.[60] And years
later, Brent Maddock compares Hulot's physical grace to Chaplin, his
deadpan to Keaton, and his innocence to Harry Langdon.[61] Similarly,
Théodore Louis likens Tati's cinematic style to that of René Clair.[62]

Along with his critics, Tati, himself, has engaged in this trans-
historical discourse. He has remarked that "inevitably . . . [a com-
ic] is compared to Chaplin" and has, himself, imagined how the Tramp
would handle the tire/wreath gag in Les Vacances.[63] Elsewhere, he
has admitted his debt to Keaton, whose anarchic Cops influenced
Playtime.[64] Moreover, Tati has situated his gradual move toward a
mass comic hero firmly within the evolution of film style. As he
says:

> The first film comic was named Little Tich.[65] He did
> a music-hall number called Big Boots, an exceptional
> number which was filmed very simply . . . It is the de-
> parture for everything which has been done in comedy.
> Afterwards, everything came from the music-hall, the
> great school of Keaton, Chaplin, Max Linder, etc. But
> comedy has evolved. After having had a character who
> presented himself before you with a label saying "I am
> the little clown of the evening, I know how to juggle,
> to be a lover, I am a musician, gagman, etc.," one
> came to Laurel and Hardy . . . Hardy being the white
> clown and Laurel being Auguste. An important evolution
> was made by them . . . both were at the same time the
> exploiter and the Auguste . . . The scheme has evolved

further and you have had the Ritz Brothers who were
three . . . Then you had the Marx Brothers: four.
Then one comes to Helzapoppin where everyone participates in the gag.[66]

And then, we might add, comes Playtime.

In most previous published discussions of the sources of Tati's
style, the American comic tradition has been decidedly favored as a
formative influence. Though Maddock duly notes the importance of
André Deed and Max Linder, he gives more attention to Chaplin, Keaton,
and others. The national roots of Tati's comedy has been a crucial
issue in the critical literature since the director's debut in the
late 1940s. In fact, many French writers seemed to champion Tati
precisely for his role in resuscitating the French comic spirit--
overpowered for decades by the American cinema. Critic Jean-Louis
Tallenay reminded his readers in 1953 that "the French cinema [had]
. . . created film comedy," and applauded Tati as its current hope.[67]
And André Bazin, in the same year, saw in Jour de fête a renaissance
of French comedy.[68]

Although these critics make valid points about Tati's ties to the
French comic tradition, there is also a hidden agenda to their commentary. For the postwar French film community felt hostility toward
the American cinema for flooding the market with its own film product,
thereby squelching the recovering native industry.[69] Hence, the critics' praise of Tati as a quintessentially French film comic bespeaks
a cultural chauvinism, as well as a genuine respect for his talent.

Jour de fête was made during this era of Franco-American tension
and, viewed in this context, becomes an extremely interesting text.
For it can be seen as a self-conscious discourse on two crucial issues of the period: the national sources of Tati's comic style and
the role of American cinema in the postwar European economy. Such a
reading hinges on one aspect of the village festival portrayed in
Jour de fête--the film tent showing an "Arizona Jim Parker" western
and a documentary on the American postal system. The latter discloses
that the American mail service (unlike François's operation) involves
impressive technology and speed. After the townsfolk view it, they
mock François for his primitive methods, and the next day he retali-
ates by setting out to do a "tour à l'Américaine." By evening, his
attempts to update the postal delivery have led to a series of comic
catastrophes, and an old village woman urges him to return to his
old-fashioned Gallic ways.

But what does this quaint, comic film have to do with the national
roots of Tati's comedy or with the role of the American cinema in
postwar France? First, it is important to note that the comic style
of Jour de fête is decidedly schizophrenic.[70] The opening sections
involve the slow-paced comedy of observation identified with Tati,
whereas the later sequences evince a more slapstick mode.

Significantly, the slapstick passages arise mostly during the "tour à l'Américaine."

By the end of the film, François has abandoned the American postal method, but his rejection goes deeper than that. For in addition, the close of Jour de fête marks Tati's rejection of the American slapstick tradition. His subsequent work discards François in favor of a more realistic comic hero and relinquishes the high-speed high jinks of Jour de fête in favor of a more distended and displaced comic style.

Jour de fête also articulates a critique of the American cinema in postwar France. Significantly, both films playing at the French village fair are American products: The Rivals of Arizona Jim and the postal documentary. Clearly, Jour de fête censures the ubiquity of American cinema—a stance that would be particularly resonant in the French film world of 1949. Within this context, one of the central gags of Jour de fête—the raising of the town flagpole and mounting of the French tricolor—seems not simply a convenient vehicle for slapstick but rather an assertion of national pride.

Recognizing Tati's place within this national tradition, the ranking of influences upon his work shifts, and certain French filmmakers come into prominence. The first is René Clair. In his book on Tati, Brent Maddock does mention certain similarities between the styles of Clair and Tati: an interest in early film form, a propensity for social satire, a minimal use of dialogue.[71] And in two earlier monographs by Théodore Louis and Geneviève Agel, Clair's name arises in discussions of Tati's films.[72] But the ties between the two directors are complex and warrant further analysis.

Central to the link between Clair and Tati is their shared sense of poetic fantasy, a spirit identified with the French comic stance. Although American humor is often fantastic—be it a cabin hovering on a precipice in Chaplin's The Gold Rush or a deaf-blind man destroying a grocery in Fields's It's a Gift (1934)—it veers toward the grotesque or violent. The French sensibility, on the other hand, runs toward whimsy—a love of the quaint or odd. It is a far gentler form of comic fantasy than the American brand, bordering on the eccentric rather than the brutal.

Precisely this sense of comic whimsy characterizes the comedy of Clair and resounds in the films of Tati. In Entr'acte (1924), for example, one sees foreshadowed certain Tatiesque moments. The comic chase of the well-dressed bourgeois after a runaway hearse is reminiscent of Hulot's encounter with a funeral party in Les Vacances. And Clair's comic troupe encircling a miniature Eiffel Tower sparks associations to the tourist group in Playtime. Similarly, there are moments in Clair's Le Million (1931) that prefigure aspects of Tati's films. (When the lovers' backstage gestures are "synchronized" to the on-stage opera, we are reminded of the scene in Jour de fête in

which a couple's flirtation is matched with the dialogue of an
American western.)

À nous la liberté, however, asserts the greatest connections between Clair and Tati. The sound technique of the film--with its
minimization of dialogue and its emphasis on music--seems a precursor
of Tati's style. Furthermore, the film's cartoonlike brand of comedy
(the scene of the singing flowers) seems preparatory for the bold sus-
pension of audiovisual realism in the films of Tati. But the thematic
connections between À nous la liberté and Tati's work are even more
significant, since the film shares with Tati's oeuvre a concern for
the issue of work and leisure. As Clair himself once noted (in a
statement worthy of Tati): "We must work in order to live, but it
is absurd to live merely in order to work."[73]

Consonant with this attitude toward leisure is Clair's passion
for preserving human liberty, be it political or spiritual. This
sense of poetic freedom is also central to the work of Tati. In response to the alienating world presented in a film like Playtime, Tati
ultimately urges the spectator to retaliate with the powers of creative vision: to transform a highway light into a bluebell, or a
traffic jam into a carousel.

Finally, Tati and Clair share a rather hostile stance to the
corporate film industry, a position often manifested directly in
their films. At the time of À nous la liberté, René Clair opposed
the coming of sound, primarily for its abridgment of artistic auton-
omy. From early on in his career, Clair had situated himself outside
the mainstream commercial cinema and had remained wary of industrial-
ists whose prime interest was the proliferation of profits and not
the creation of an art form. When sound came in, Clair was outraged
that those who knew nothing of cinematic art had the power to so
radically transform cinematic practice. As he put it:

> What is cinema for us? A new medium of expression,
> a new poetry and dramaturgy. What is it for them?
> Fifty thousand theatres all over the world that must
> be supplied with a show--film, music, variety acts,
> or a sheep with five legs--capable of making the
> spectator's money pour into the box office.[74]

The coming of sound must also have represented to Clair the adop-
tion of an expensive technology that would make independent filmmaking significantly more difficult. Whatever problems avant-garde
filmmakers faced in the silent era were thus accentuated by the arrival of sound.

Given this context, the narrative of À nous la liberté takes on
added significance. When the character of Louis (Raymond Cordy) es-
capes prison and becomes a corrupt corporate executive, he does so in
the guise of a phonograph record manufacturer--a sign of Clair's

hostility to the talkies. Furthermore, when it is recalled that one of the most powerful film producers in France (Léon Gaumont) was responsible for pioneering sound-on-disc, the film takes on added meaning.[75]

Recognizing this apparent self-reflexivity in À nous la liberté, it is easy to see the ideological parallels between Clair and Tati, both of whom view themselves as independent film artisans. Thus the tone of À nous la liberté bears comparison to Jour de fête and Trafic: two parables of the artist's plight in the commercial film industry. Given this relationship between Clair and Tati, it is not surprising that the former embraced the latter as his heir apparent. In a 1958 interview, Clair referred to Tati as his "spiritual son," and said, "He is doing the things I had to stop doing thirty years ago when sound came in."[76]

Another important predecessor of Tati is Jean Vigo, the great avant-garde filmmaker of the twenties and thirties. Ties to Vigo are, however, more tenuous than those to Clair, since Vigo is not generally thought to have worked in the comic mode. One of the most interesting connections between the two directors is revealed through a comparative analysis of À propos de Nice (1929–30) and Les Vacances.[77] Both films are satires of French seaside resorts: the former the glamorous Nice, and the latter the ordinary "X-Sur-Mer." Though Vigo's film is far more class-conscious than Tati's, both mock bourgeois leisure rituals and end in a fantasy of destruction.

Two other Vigo films bear comparison to works by Tati. Jean Taris (1930–31), a short study of a champion swimmer, is relevant to Tati's fascination with sports. More central is Zero de conduite (1933), a whimsical story of students oppressed at a French boarding school. In its sympathy with young boys victimized by a repressive educational system, the film bears relation to Mon oncle. Furthermore, the fanciful figure of the teacher Huguet is reminiscent of the character of Hulot: for just as Hulot offers a liberated role model to his nephew Gérard, so does Huguet to the boarding school boys. At one point in Zero de conduite, Huguet does an imitation of Charlie Chaplin--or Charlot as the French would call him. One would like to believe that Tati's name for Hulot derived from a composite of Huguet and Charlot.

Another important French influence on the films of Tati is the work of the brothers Prevert--Jacques, as scenarist, and Pierre, as director. Their most interesting film from this perspective is Le Voyage surprise, made in 1946. Set in a small French town, it tells the tale of a charming old gentleman, Grandpa Piuff, who decides to organize "mystery tours" for his neighbors. Such trips involve a voyage of unspecified itinerary, with people enlisting for an adventure into the unknown. Grandpa Piuff's trips stand in direct opposition to those of M. Grosbois, which take people to predictable tourist spots like museums and monuments. Clearly in its satire on tourism, the film presages Playtime and, in its valorization of "mystery" in

everyday life, participates in the liberating poetic thrust of
French film comedy.

The Enchanted Domain

> The realm of the funny is infinite.
> Yet we use funny in one sense that
> gives a useful clue. We use it to
> mean odd, unusual, strange, condi-
> tions that may not be laughable at
> all; indeed the phrase "that is
> funny" can hint danger.[78]
>
> --Robert Heilman

> Jacques Tati has a feeling for
> comedy, because he has a feeling
> for strangeness.[79]
>
> --Jean-Luc Godard

As part of the French comic tradition, the work of Tati participates in a unique aesthetic, one that seems tied to a particular
movement in French cultural history--surrealism of the 1920s. And
it is surely no accident that several major figures of the French
comic cinema (René Clair, Jean Vigo, Jacques Prevert) traveled in
surrealist circles. But what precisely do the comedies of Clair,
Vigo, Tati, and the brothers Prevert have in common with the surrealist ethic or aesthetic?

An examination of their surface visual style generates few affinities. Films like À nous la liberté, Zero de conduite, or Le
Voyage surprise display none of the odd, disjunctive strategies of a
painting by Dali or a film by Luis Buñuel. Yet the tone of these
comedies, with their note of oddity, shares with surrealist works a
sense of the bizarre underside of quotidian bourgeois life. There
are, for instance, the grotesque masks in À Propos de Nice or various
scenes in Zero de conduite: the dormitory revolt with its weird slow-
motion procession or the school graduation with its queer dummy figures of parents, teachers, and town officials. Thus, these filmmakers,
like the surrealists, reveal the Psychopathology of Everyday Life.

French comic cinema also shares with surrealism certain basic as-
sumptions and themes. Both evince a belief in the importance of individual liberty in opposition to social repression. And both valorize
irrationality and imagination as the wellsprings of true revolt.
Finally, both place their faith in the power of comedy to activate
such a psychic rebellion. Hence, the surrealists' love of American
slapstick movies becomes comprehensible, as does Anton Artaud's
praise of the Marx Brothers for presenting "a kind of boiling anarchy,
a kind of disintegration of the essence of the real by poetry."[80] The
films of Tati participate in this broad sensibility. Though far from
surrealist projects in any classical sense of the term, his films

benefit from the legacy of a surrealist perspective.

On an aesthetic level, Tati's films also inherit from surrealism a profound sense of the strange—a feature noted perceptively by Jean-Luc Godard. Others have remarked on this quality as well: Jean-André Fieschi, for example, has described how gags in Tati's films often "lose all funniness only to gain in pure strangeness."[81] But while critics have mentioned the strange aura of Tati's work, it has not been accorded the proper status of a major contribution to comic form nor tied emphatically to the surrealist tradition.[82]

In pursuing this issue, it is useful to discuss the work of a particular surrealist artist, René Magritte, a Belgian painter who lived in Paris in the 1920s. Though no evidence exists for a historical link between Tati and Magritte, an examination of the painter's style can elucidate certain aspects of Tati's films.

First, the surface look of Tati's films at times sparks associations to the work of Magritte. The opening shots of Playtime (centering on the blue Parisian sky) are reminiscent of that iconography in Magritte's: "The False Mirror" (1958), "The Six Elements" (1928), "On the Threshold of Liberty" (1929), "Wasted Effort" (1962), or "Personal Values" (1952). The crisp, superficial realism of Tati and Magritte's imagery seems to communicate a false complacency concerning the stability of the "real" world.

Moreover, in both artists' work, there is a play on illusionary surfaces: for Magritte, the painted canvas, and for Tati, the reflecting plane of glass. One recalls Magritte's "The Human Condition I" (1933) in which a painting of a landscape stands in front of an open window, obliterating the real scene. Reminiscent of this is a sequence in Playtime, in which M. Hulot pursues a reflection of the elusive M. Giffard which has come to substitute for the man himself.

In both the work of Magritte and Tati there is also a shared interest in the dynamics of word and image and the ironies such a relationship engenders. One thinks of Magritte's "The Use of Words I" (1928-29) where a linguistic statement about a pipe seemingly contradicts the image, or of "The Key of Dreams" (1920) in which pictures of objects are matched with the "wrong" words. Although the films of Tati evince no extended discourse on language and image, they do frequently demonstrate a sense of visual/linguistic play. In Playtime, it is the word Paris—captured on the airport sign and the highway asphalt—that "stands for" the true city, a locale the tourists never really grasp. A more complex word/image trope occurs during Playtime's final carousel sequence. Through a window being washed, the viewer glimpses the massive traffic jam encircling the roundabout. In center frame is an ice-cream wagon, labeled glace. Shortly thereafter, a shot occurs of the windowpane reflecting the American tourists in their bus. As the window washer tilts the pane up and down, the tourists yell "ooh" and "ah," as though they too were being tipped.

Significantly, this play on the window's reflecting surface has been cued in by the sign glace, a pun on the English word glass. Finally, there is the poster for Trafic that decorated the entrance to the theater into which it opened. On a mirrored surface, bearing the name of the film, was reflected the Parisian traffic--buses, motor-cycles, and cars. Thus, a pictorial/linguistic joke was created, with the worlds of representation and reality confused.[83]

Beyond these similarities of imagery in the work of Tati and Magritte, there is also a shared sensibility. Magritte has always displayed a strong love of comedy, as is clear from such titles as "The Comic Spirit" (1927) and "Homage to Mack Sennett" (1934). Furthermore, he was evidently an avid fan of slapstick movies and even made some short comic films.[84] Fundamental to his sense of humor is a fondness for the paradox which is apparent in many of his canvasses. "Les Vacances de Hegel" (1958), for example, depicts an open umbrella on top of which is perched a glass of water--clearly, a subject of comic contradiction. As critic James Thrall Solby has pointed out, the work "typifies Magritte's deliciously subversive wit in that an umbrella supports a tumbler full of the water it is meant to repel."[85]

This painting is interesting in relation to Tati for several reasons. First, the title is reminiscent of Les Vacances de Monsieur Hulot, and the object depicted is one identified with the Tati persona. Beyond these seemingly accidental parallels, however, the sense of ironic paradox manifest in the Magritte painting is one that abounds in the work of Tati. There is his paradoxical use of glass in Playtime--a medium known for transparency but capable of presenting an opaque reflecting surface (like the eye in Magritte's "The False Mirror"). There is also his paradoxical view of leisure, be it a vacation at the Hotel de la Plage (modeled on the workaday world) or the international tour (which transports Americans to mirror-image European cities). Finally, there is the irony of the urban traffic jams in Playtime and Trafic, where vehicles of locomotion grind to a dead halt.

Magritte and Tati also share an interest in domestic space as the potential site of drama. One thinks of Magritte's "Now, You Don't" (1927), in which a man reading a newspaper mysteriously disappears over the course of four quasi-cinematic frames. In "Voice of Silence" (1928), Magritte presents a hauntingly empty room imbued with a dormant sense of suspense. Both these works spark associations to Les Vacances where vacationers inhabit the vacuous Hotel de la Plage parlor in a state of suspended animation--as though waiting for something to happen.

But perhaps the most intriguing aspect of Magritte's work from the perspective of Tati is his creation of the "bowler-hatted man." In the 1964 painting of that name, as well as in numerous pieces from the twenties through the sixties, Magritte populates his canvasses with a rather average-looking gentleman, wearing a bowler hat.

Sometimes several men of the same anonymous description appear in a single picture. One thinks of "Pandora's Box" (1951), "The Masterpiece or the Mysteries of the Horizon" (1955), "The Time of the Harvest" (1959), "The Great War" (1964), or "The Spirit of Adventure" (1960). Most interesting of all, is "Golconda" (1953) where myraid bowler-hatted men rain down from the sky.

But what does this Magritte persona have to do with the films of Jacques Tati? On a historical level, the two seem unrelated, and no tie between them may exist. But on an intertextual plane, the bowler-hatted man can be viewed as a surrealist alter ego of Hulot. He is a faceless individual, frequently portrayed from behind. Encased in a vacuum of silence, he seems forever posed as though frozen in a gesture of paralysis. As a distanced participant in daily life, he floats through scenes of bourgeois existence with affectless grace. He is a quintessential observer figure: in "The Time of Harvest," several bowler-hatted men peer through an open window. He is, moreover, an individual deeply marked by the industrial age. In his infinitely repeatable embodiments, he seems a transposition of assembly-line practice to the human form.[86]

These traits of the bowler-hatted man seem relevant to the character of Hulot: his loneliness, his passivity, his silence, his immobility, his eccentric normalcy, his mechanical demeanor, and his profound indirection. Even his multiple incarnations have a bearing on a film like Playtime where Tati stocks the narrative with several Hulot "doubles." In this regard, a comment made by Tati, concerning his music-hall days in London, takes on added meaning. He recalls:

> Everyday I travelled from Charing Cross to St. John's
> Lewisham. I wanted to look English; I wore a hard
> hat, a "melon"; everybody in the train smoked a pipe,
> so I bought one too.[87]

Given these parallels between the sensibilities of Magritte and Tati, it seems fitting that in 1949 Tati performed at the casino of Knokke-le-Zoute (Belgium), where Magritte would later paint the mural, "The Enchanted Domain."[88]

What this discussion of Magritte and Tati has revealed is a shared sense of the uncanny in both their work. As we know from Freud's essay on the subject, such a sentiment can involve a perception of the terrifying in the familiar, of the inanimate in the living, or of a doubling process in human existence.[89] Although in the work of Magritte, these uncanny elements retain a horrifying aura, in the films of Tati, they are transformed by the comic mode. Hence, uncanny situations become _funny_ in Heilman's dual sense of the term--both bizarre and humorous.

In summary, it is clear that Jacques Tati's contribution to the comic tradition is a significant and complex one. Although borrowing from the French and American schools, he brought a uniquely modernist effect to the ancient genre. This aesthetic is evident both in the innovative structure of Tati's films and in their sense of the strange. As opposed to the raucous burlesque of the Keystone Kops, the tendentious caricature of Charlie Chaplin, the grotesque hyperbole of the Marx Brothers, or the placid whimsy of Clair, Vigo, and Prevert—the comic tone of Tati's films shares more with the modernist aesthetic of a dramatist like Harold Pinter, a dancer like Murray Louis, or a painter like René Magritte.

Finally, the eccentricity of Tati's films serves a profoundly didactic function, rooted in his comic theory and style. For it ultimately enables him to teach his audience to see, in a manner previously unknown to them. As the critic Victor Shklovsky once remarked, art can restore to us the very "sensation of life," by rendering the universe "unfamiliar"—by making our world decidedly "strange."[90]

NOTES

1. Vincent Canby, "Godard—The Revolutionary as Revelation," New York Times, 1 June 1980.

2. Henry Ford, My Life and Work (New York: Garden City Publishing Co., 1972), p. 90.

3. Brent Maddock, The Films of Jacques Tati, p. 113 (entry 312).

4. Gerald Mast, The Comic Mind, p. 294 (entry 260).

5. Armand Cauliez, Jacques Tati, p. 16 (entry 192). My translation.

6. Noël Carroll, "An In-Depth Analysis of Buster Keaton's The General," Ph.D. dissertation, New York University, 1976.

7. Tati in Cauliez, Tati, p. 87 (entry 192). My translation.

8. Tati in Cauliez, Tati, pp. 117-18 (entry 150). My translation.

9. Max Horkheimer and Theodor Adorno, The Dialectics of Enlightenment (New York: Seabury Press, 1972).

10. Tati in Penelope Gilliatt, Jacques Tati, p. 59 (entry 292).

11. Théodore Louis, Jacques Tati, p. 13 (entry 144).

12. Tati in "For Variety: Automation, Insanity and War" (entry 86).

13. Henri Bergson, "Laughter," in Comedy, ed. Wylie Sypher (New York: Doubleday/Anchor, 1956), p. 84.

14. Antoine de Saint-Exupery, Terre des hommes (Paris: Gallimard, 1939), p. 58.

15. See Maddock, Tati, p. 113 (entry 312).

16. Tati in "Voyage à Tativille," p. 19 (entry 157). My transla-
    tion.

17. Werner Heisenberg, "The Representation of Nature in
    Contemporary Physics," in The Discontinuous Universe, ed.
    Sallie Sears and Georgiana Lord (New York: Basic Books,
    1972), p. 131.

18. Tati in Gilliatt, "Profiles: Playing," p. 40 (entry 256).

19. Tati in "For Variety: Automation, Insanity and War," (entry
    86).

20. René Guyonnet, "Le XI festival de Cannes," (entry 111).

21. Tati in Gilliatt, Tati, p. 23 (entry 292).

22. Tati in André Bazin and François Truffaut, "Entretien avec
    Jacques Tati," p. 16 (entry 95).

23. Bergson, "Laughter," p. 73 and p. 187.

24. Roy Armes, "Jacques Tati," p. 155 (entry 158).

25. Tati in Bazin and Truffaut, "Entretien," p. 5 (entry 95). My
    translation.

26. See Moses Hadas, ed., The Complete Plays of Aristophanes (New
    York: Bantam Books, 1972), p. 7.

27. Joel Siegel, "Playtime," p. 40 (entry 277).

28. Tati in Gilliatt, Tati, p. 69 (entry 292).

29. Tati in Martine Monod, "Jacques Tati ou le passioné rais-
    sonable," pp. 1, 5 (entry 80). My translation.

30. Tati in Cauliez, Tati, p. 92 (entry 192). My translation.

31. Ibid.

32. Tati in Jonathan Rosenbaum, "Paris Journal," p. 4 (entry 225).

33. Rosenbaum, "Tati's Democracy" (entry 263).

34. Tati in Gilliatt, "Profiles," p. 38 (entry 256).

35. Sigmund Freud, Jokes and Their Relation to the Unconscious,
    edited by James Strachey (New York: Norton, 1960).

36. Jean-André Fieschi, "Jacques Tati," p. 1000 (entry 334).

37. James Sully, An Essay on Laughter (London: Longmans, Green &
    Co., 1902), p. 344.

38. Bergson, "Laughter," p. 111.

39. Ben Shahn, The Shape of Content (Cambridge, Mass.: Harvard
    University Press, 1957), p. 65.

40. André Bazin articulates this position in "The Evolution of the
    Language of Cinema," in What Is Cinema? translated by Hugh
    Gray (Berkeley: University of California Press, 1970).

41. Tati in "Tati," p. 11 (entry 188). My translation.

42. Tati in "Tati," p. 15 (entry 188). My translation.

43. Siegfried Giedion, Mechanization Takes Command (New York: Norton, 1969), p. 32

44. Tati in Kevin Thomas, "Jacques Tati: Silent Comedy's Heir" (entry 245).

45. Charles Walker and Robert Guest, The Man on the Assembly Line (Cambridge, Mass.: Harvard University Press, 1952), p. 12.

46. This issue is more fully discussed in Lucy Fischer, "Beyond Freedom and Dignity" (entry 291).

47. This issue is discussed more fully in Lucy Fischer, "Homo Ludens: An Analysis of Four Films by Jacques Tati" (entry 319).

48. Bergson, "Laughter," p. 105. My italics.

49. Raymond Durgnat, The Crazy Mirror (New York: Dell, 1969), p. 35. My italics.

50. Pierre Baudry, "Sur le réalisme," p. 40 (entry 212). My translation.

51. Tati mentions this in Jean-Jacques Henry and Serge Le Péron, "Entretien avec Tati" (entry 330).

52. Bazin, "M. Hulot et le temps," p. 122 (entry 203). See also entry 31, entry 340, and the Appendix for a translation of the essay.

53. Tati in Cauliez, Tati, p. 106 (entry 192). My translation.

54. Tati in "Tati," p. 15 (entry 188). My translation.

55. Paulette Pellenq, "Sur Playtime" (entry 183).

56. Fieschi, "Tati," p. 1004 (entry 334).

57. See entries 188-89, 326, 328-29, 330, 332.

58. Fieschi, "Tati," p. 1005 (entry 334). My translation.

59. Tati in Cauliez, Tati, p. 102 (entry 192). My translation.

60. Geneviève Agel, Hulot Parmi Nous, p. 20 (entry 62).

61. Maddock, Tati, pp. 17 and 19 (entry 312).

62. Louis, Tati, p. 8 (entry 144).

63. Tati in "The Cinema According to Tati," p. 155 (entry 339).

64. Tati in "Tati," p. 12 (entry 188).

65. Tati is referring to a French turn-of-the-century comic vaudeville performer (recorded on film), whose act involved his wearing huge "slap-shoes." The Museum of Modern Art in New York City has footage of Little Tich in their archive on the reel "Cinéma parlant en 1900."

66. Tati in "Tati," p. 8 (entry 188). My translation.

67. Jean-Louis Tallenay, "Les Français n'ont-ils pas la tête comique?" p. 56 (entry 46).

68. Bazin, "M. Hulot," p. 110 (entry 203).

69. Specifically, the French film community was upset by the Blum-Byrnes agreement of May 1946 which annulled pre-World War II quotas of dubbed American films allowed for release in France. The agreement resulted in a glut of American films on the market. [See Georges Sadoul, French Film (London: Falcon Press, 1952), pp. 109-10.]

70. Louis, Tati, p. 7 (entry 144).

71. Maddock, Tati, pp. 27-28 (entry 312).

72. Agel, Hulot, p. 19 (entry 62) and Louis, Tati, p. 9 (entry 144).

73. René Clair, À nous la liberté and Entr'acte (New York: Simon & Schuster, 1970), p. 9.

74. René Clair, Cinema Yesterday and Today (New York: Dover, 1972), p. 129.

75. Leslie Halliwell, "Jacques Tati," p. 289 (entry 208).

76. René Clair in Richard Wald, "René Clair and the Silent Era," New York Herald Tribune, 30 November 1958.

77. Raymond Jean, "Les Couleurs de la vie," p. 48 (entry 54).

78. Robert Heilman, The Ways of the World (Seattle and London: University of Washington Press, 1972), p. 18.

79. Jean-Luc Godard in Fieschi, "Tati," p. 1003 (entry 334).

80. Anton Artaud in Durgnat, Crazy Mirror, p. 150.

81. Fieschi, "Tati," p. 1004 (entry 334).

82. The issue of surrealism is mentioned by Louis in Tati, p. 12 (entry 144).

83. Octave Burnett, "Fiche filmographique #553: Trafic," pp. 17-23 (entry 214).

84. Louis Scutenaire, "La Fidélité des images--René Magritte--Le Cinématographe et la photographie," (Bruxelles: Belgian Government, 1976), pp. 68-70.

85. James Thrall Solby, Magritte (New York: Museum of Modern Art, 1965), p. 19.

86. This idea came up in a discussion with my colleague Dr. James Knapp of the University of Pittsburgh.

87. Tati in Harold Woodside, "Tati Speaks," p. 7 (entry 204).

88. According to Cauliez in <u>Tati</u>, p. 8 (entry 192), Tati appeared there in 1949. According to A. M. Hammacher in <u>Magritte</u> (New York: Abrams, 1974), p. 64, "The Enchanted Domain" was commissioned in 1951 and completed in 1953.

89. Sigmund Freud, "The Uncanny," in <u>On Creativity and the Unconscious</u> (New York: Harper & Row, 1958), pp. 122-61.

90. Victor Shklovsky, "Art as Technique," in <u>Russian Formalist Criticism: Four Essays</u>, ed. Lee T. Lemon and Marion Reis (Lincoln: University of Nebraska Press, 1965), p. 12 and footnote on p. 4.

III. The Films: Synopses, Credits, and Notes

Note: The early short films of Jacques Tati are not available in commercial distribution, and only a few are preserved in French archives. Some of those exist only in negative prints and are, therefore, not available for screening. Plot synopses, therefore, are based on discussions of these films in various texts.

*1   OSCAR, CHAMPION DE TENNIS (1931-32)

Synopsis

This short comic film serves as a vehicle for Tati's performance of his tennis sports mime, one which later reappears in the tennis sequence of Les Vacances de Monsieur Hulot.

Credits

Director: Jacques Tati
Screenplay: Jacques Tati
Cast: Jacques Tati
Running time: Short film
Note: According to Armand Cauliez (entry 192, p. 7), the film was never actually completed.

*2   ON DEMANDE UNE BRUTE (1934)

Synopsis

"The brute is Tati who by chance, despite his will and wishes, wins a competition and is given the title of a fighter. This brute is as sweet as a lamb and under the thumb of a shrewish wife. In the ring, his first reaction of a déclassé sportsman is to gallop off a hundred meters with his rival in pursuit. True, one is obliged to recall Charlie the Boxer or Charlie and Fatty in the Ring. [It is not clear what films are referred to here, but they are likely The Champion (1915) and The Knockout (1914).] But more than anything, one is witness here to the fascinating birth of an absolutely new comic character: awkward, ungainly, bizarre, not knowing what to do with his huge body. He barely manages to squeeze it into

59

the frame of the screen, and that through many contortions and heroic flounderings. He takes refuge subsequently in a kind of morose contemplation, a dreamy solitude which links him more closely (if one must have reference points) to Buster Keaton or to Harry Langdon rather than to Charlie. For the essence of Tati's comedy is not farce, nor clowning, but rather a kind of complacent delectation, a sort of semi-vegetative un-consciousness, which makes him totally without responsibility for what happens to him, and which, as a consequence of this maladaptation, betrays a profound bitterness. One notes also in this film the unusual sequence of a family meal, where the sardines travel from the goldfish bowl, and vice versa. The gag is executed with great understatement, without jolts or clashes. These are already the 'games of humor and of chance' which Geneviève Agel will take pleasure in describing to us." (From Beylie, entry 78, pp. 12-13, translated by Channa Weyel)

Credits

Director:	Charles Barrois
Assistant director:	René Clément
Screenplay:	Jacques Tati and Alfred Sauvy
Cast:	Jacques Tati and a wrestling champion
Running time:	Short film

*3   GAI DIMANCHE (1935)

Synopsis

"Tati appears in [this film] as a luckless dandy, sort of a tramp (but dressed with a certain elegance) who at the start of the film is expelled from the mouth of the métro where he has spent the night. He allows himself to be dragged by one of his friends (a streethawker) to a picnic. They take off in a rented, wobbly, open cab, which is also occupied by a troup of weirdos summoned by the call of the two plotters' accomplices. Following some mechanical and gastronomical episodes of various types, the day ends in a disorderly flight.

The direction [of the film] is perfectly ordinary, since Tati did not have the good fortune to find a Mack Sennett. Yet one can already see emerge, however timidly, the future character of the scatter-brain, tossed about by events, moving lazily with the wind, as would the arrow on a one-way sign, transformed into a weathervane.

Likewise, one cannot help but notice in this "voyage sur-prise" which winds across fields (with Tati standing at the front of the car surveying the horizon with his innocent look) a curious resemblance to the voyage which, many years later, will be organized by M. Hulot's commander. In addition, the fleeting presence of two children, one locked up inside a car where he imitates the sounds of the motor, and the other suddenly interrupting a performance of magic tricks by breaking, with a backhand motion, the egg hidden in the magician's pocket, allows us to make still more eloquent comparisons between this and the later works.

Another scene, where a young girl, standing on a mound plays a trumpet (which on the sound track is heard as a hunting horn) while around her adults are chasing a chicken destined to become their lunch, seems to be already a beautiful idea characteristic of Tati. And finally, the sound accompaniment as a whole, composed of digestive tract sounds and of animals croaking, announces directly Hulot's audio-visual structure." (From Beylie, entry 78, pp. 11-12, translated by Channa Weyel)

Credits

Producer:	Atlantic Films (O. M. de Andria)
Director:	Jacques Berr
Screenplay:	Jacques Tati and the clown, Rhum
Cast:	Jacques Tati and Rhum
Running time:	33 minutes

*4   SOIGNE TON GAUCHE (1936)

Synopsis

"This film is a vehicle for Tati's boxing sports mime. Tati plays the role of a farmhand who observes a champion boxer in training. He then proceeds to imitate him and cause a string of mishaps and gags." (From Cauliez, entry 192, p. 7)

"Everything here is stamped 'in filigree,' the authenticity of the natural country decor, which will be one of the great daring features of Jour de fête; the amateurish and improvised aspect of the business resembling a good joke between pals; the solitary pantomime in the 'grange' barn of the farm boy boxing with an invisible adversary, which symbolizes all the spirit of Tati's withdrawn, repressed fighter; the striped sweater made of the same material as Hulot's socks; the mailman, a picturesque rough draft, drawn with an already self-assured stroke; finally the spirit of childhood, represented by kids making movies with a coffee mill--we find again in their embryonic state all the themes which will be subsequently developed, this time without any possible retrospective illusion." (From Beylie, entry 78, p. 13, translated by Channa Weyel)

Credits

Producer:	Fred Orain (Cady-Films)

Director:	René Clément
Screenplay:	Jacques Tati
Music:	Jean Yatove
Cast:	Jacques Tati
Running time:	20 minutes

*5   RETOUR À LA TERRE (1938)

Synopsis

No synopsis available.

Credits

Producer:	Jacques Tati
Director:	Jacques Tati
Screenplay:	Jacques Tati
Cast:	Jacques Tati
Running time:	Short film

*6   L'ÉCOLE DES FACTEURS (1947)

Synopsis

Tati takes the role of François, the postman, in this comedy of French village life. This short film was later expanded into Jour de fête. (See synopsis below.)

Credits

Producer:	Cady-Films
Director:	Jacques Tati
Screenplay:	Jacques Tati
Assistant director:	Henri Marquet
Photography:	Louis Felix
Music:	Jean Yatove
Directorial assistants:	J. Cottin and H. Gansser
Supervision/Direction:	Fred Orain
Cast:	Jacques Tati
Running time:	18 minutes

Note: This film received the Prix Max Linder (1949) for short comic films, and the Inventaire Du Cinéma (1949).

7   JOUR DE FÊTE (1949)

Synopsis

Jour de fête takes place in a small French village on the day of the annual carnival. The film opens with the arrival in town of the merry-go-round truck, and we see real horses in the field shy away at the sight of their wooden "brothers." Children run down the road in glee, and an old townswoman observes the events. In town, preparations for the festival are being made. The cafe owner has just painted his chairs, and many predicaments arise because they are not yet dry. The town crier rather ineffectually makes an announcement, and a group of men try unsuccessfully to raise the town flagpole. In the midst of this activity, a romance blossoms between a young village girl and Roger, the merry-go-round owner.

The focus of the film then shifts to the character of François, the town postman, whom we encounter on his bicycle having problems with a bee. Eventually he rides into town, narrowly missing the toppling flagpole and offers to help the townsmen set up the flagpole, occasioning numerous gags. The film then follows François on his postal rounds. He jovially delivers a telegram to a man, but fails to notice the corpse laid out on the bed; he looks backward while riding his bicycle and manages to get it caught in the harness of a wagon; he gestures while holding a hose for someone and manages to douse everyone in sight.

Meanwhile, in town the festivities proceed: the marching band plays, even as the cymbalist attempts to use his instrument to swat a bee; children dressed in their Sunday finest stroll expectantly into town; people play various carnival games. As part of the festival, a tent has been set up as an ersatz cinema. A friend beckons François to the cinema to see a documentary film on the modern American postal system, which utilizes helicopters, mechanical mail sorters, and other up-to-date equipment.

Leaving the cinema, the villagers are impressed with what they have seen and begin to tease François about his old-fashioned methods. Dejected, François gets drunk. The next day, the traveling carnival makes preparations to leave town. Before they go, however, the merry-go-round operators advise François to speed up his postal delivery "like an American." Scenes follow of François speeding down the road, jumping on and off his bicycle, talking on the telephone while riding his bike, using the back of a moving truck to sort his mail, delivering letters in a rather improbable manner.

Ultimately, François's attempts at efficiency and modernization lead to a more chaotic system of mail delivery. At the end of the day, François encounters the old townswoman who has appeared periodically throughout the film. She tells him to go back to his own way of doing things, that people can "wait a few extra minutes for their letters." The film closes with the traveling fair leaving town and François learning to return to his customary French way of delivering the mail.

Credits

Producer:	Fred Orain (Cady-Films)
Director:	Jacques Tati

Screenplay:	Jacques Tati and Henri Marquet in collaboration with René Wheeler
Adapted by:	René Wheeler
Dialogue:	Jacques Tati and Henri Marquet
Photography:	J. Mercanton and M. Franchi
Cameramen:	Citovitch Mauride
Music:	Jean Yatove
Designer:	René Moulaert
Editor:	Marcel Moureau
Cast:	Jacques Tati (François), Guy Decomble (Roger, the merry-go-round owner), Paul Frankeur (Marcel, a circus assistant), Santa Relli (Roger's wife), Maine Valée (Jeanette), Roger Rafal (the barber), Beauvais (the cafe owner), Delcassen (the cinema operator), the inhabitants of Sainte-Sévère-Sur-Indre
Location:	Sainte-Sévère-Sur-Indre
Running time:	90 minutes
English version:	The Big Day, released in 1952. Prepared by Borah Minnevitch and released by Arthur Mayer and Edward Kingsley.

Note: The film was originally shot in two forms. A color negative was made in the Thomson Color process, and a traditional black-and-white negative was shot as well. However, due to laboratory error, only the black-and-white negative was processed. When Tati rereleased the film in 1961 (at the Olympia Theatre), he made a new print of the film and hand-stenciled some of the color effects that he had hoped to achieve in the earlier version. The film received the following awards: Venice Festival Award for the Best Scenario (1949); Grand Prix Du Cinéma (1950); International Critics Award, Cannes (1953); Louis Delluc Award (1953); Femina Award, Brussels (1953).

8   LES VACANCES DE MONSIEUR HULOT (1953)

Synopsis

As the title indicates, Les Vacances de Monsieur Hulot is about a vacation at a French, middle-class, seaside resort, the Hotel de la Plage. The film opens with sequences of various people traveling to the hotel: vacationers taking a train, and M. Hulot driving to the seashore in his broken-down, puttering old car. The camera focuses on a young woman, Martine, who is among the vacationers boarding the train.

The next sequence of the film concerns the arrival of guests at the hotel. Martine is seen unpacking her suitcase. After all the other guests arrive and are seated in the hotel parlor, Hulot pulls up in his noisy car, the backfires disturbing the peace. Each time he opens the hotel door to bring in his luggage, he either bumps into someone or upsets the order of the room by letting in a gust of air. The guests retire to the dining room for lunch; Hulot arrives late.

The next day, the vacationers are seen at the beach. A young child unfastens a winch and a boat slides into the water; Hulot, who stands nearby, is suspected. Another meal takes place in which Hulot continually upsets the man at his table by reaching across him to grab some food. Later that afternoon, Martine's aunt arrives at the seashore. Hulot, who is already fond of Martine, helps unload her aunt's luggage, but manages to trip and hurl himself through the woman's house. That evening, while other guests sit sedately in the hotel parlor, Hulot joins some campers in drink for a noisy party.

On another day, we see Hulot upset a group of people exercising on the beach and later attempt unsuccessfully to paint a canoe. Then, rather sheepishly, he tracks up the floor of the hotel lobby with his muddy shoes. Later in the day, Hulot and a fellow vacationer go out for a ride, but Hulot lands them in the midst of a cemetery burial.

On another day, Hulot is seen playing tennis, but he unnerves the guests with his unconventional tennis form. That evening, Hulot plays Ping-Pong in the hotel parlor with a young boy and disturbs the other guests who are concentrating on their bridge games.

On still another day, Hulot attempts to go horseback riding with Martine, but encounters problems with his unruly horse. On the night of the hotel's masked ball, Hulot arrives in a pirate's costume, finding Martine and a few children as the only other masqueraders. Another day, Hulot drives some guests to the hotel picnic, but, characteristically, has a flat tire on the way.

On one of the last evenings of the holiday, Hulot is chased by a dog into an old shed. He lights a match to give himself some light and manages to set off a blitzkrieg of fireworks which awaken the hotel inhabitants. On the final vacation day, as guests leave, most snub the eccentric M. Hulot. However, certain people (like Martine, an old henpecked man, an English woman) let Hulot know that they have enjoyed his company and that he has brightened their holiday. M. Hulot departs and his old wreck of a car backfires down the road.

Credits

Producer: Fred Orain (Cady Films) in

	collaboration with Discina, and Éclair-Journal.
Director:	Jacques Tati
Screenplay:	Jacques Tati and Henri Marquet with the collaboration of P. Aubert and J. Lagrange.
Photography:	Jacques Mercanton and Jean Mousselle
Art direction:	Henri Marquet
Set decoration:	R. Briancourt and H. Schmitt
Music:	Alains Romans
Editors:	Grassi, Gimon Bretoneiche, Suzanne Baron
Production manager:	Phillipe Schwob
Production director:	Fred Orain
Cameramen:	Pierre Ancrenaz, Fabien Toriman, André Marquette
Cast:	Jacques Tati (M. Hulot), Nathalie Pascaud (Martine), Louis Perrault (Fred), Michèle Rolla (Martine's aunt), André Dubois (the commandant), Suzy Willy (the wife of the commandant), Valentine Camax (the English woman), Lucien Frégis (the hotel owner), Marguerite Gérard (the promenading woman), René Lacourt (the promenading man), Raymond Carl (the boy), Michèle Brabo (a woman vacationer), Georges Adlin (the South American)
Locations:	The interiors were shot at the studios at Boulogne-Billancourt. The exteriors were filmed in Britanny at Saint-Mar-Sur-Mer, near Saint-Nazaire.
Running time:	90 minutes
English version:	Mr. Hulot's Holiday

Note: The film won the following awards: Prix de la Critique Internationale, Cannes (1953); Prix Louis Delluc (1953); Prix Femina (1953); Prix De L'Union Algerienne Des Critiques De Film (1953); Second Prize for Best Foreign Film of the Year, Sweden (1954); Best Film of the Year, Cuba (1956); Nomination for the Academy Award for Best Scenario (1956).

9   MON ONCLE (1958)

Synopsis

Mon oncle concerns Hulot's relations with his sister, brother-in-law, and nephew—the Arpel family. The Arpels live in a sterile, modern, French suburb, where homes are replete with all the latest mechanical gadgets: electric garage doors,

mechanical fountains, automated kitchens, and so on. Though
M. and Mme. Arpel are delighted with their life-style, their
son Gérard seems bored with his geometrically designed surroundings and the clocklike routine of the household. He
looks forward to his weekly visits with his whimsical uncle,
M. Hulot, with whom he is always sure to have a good time.

Unlike the Arpels, Hulot lives in the old part of town,
where people gather in the street to talk, and shop at the
local outdoor market. Hulot, who chooses not to work, hangs
out at the neighborhood bistro, Chez Margot. M. Arpel, who
owns a plastics factory, decides that his brother-in-law
should have a job and sets up an interview for him at another
plant. That interview turns out to be a disaster, when Hulot
tracks limestone footprints into the personnel manager's office, and the latter mistakes the accidental occurrence for
juvenile antics.

Meanwhile, at the Arpel home, Hulot's sister decides that
her brother should be married and begins to arrange a party
to introduce him to an eligible neighbor lady. That evening,
Hulot visits the Arpel home and brings Gérard a toy puppet
that delights him more than the fancy mechanical train that
his father has brought him. When Hulot goes into the kitchen
to get a drink, he has trouble with all the electrical gadgets
that the Arpels have installed.

Another day, Hulot picks Gérard up from school and, on the
way home, lets him engage in some mischievous pranks with the
neighborhood boys. A few days later, the Arpels have a garden
party to introduce Hulot to their single, neighbor. The party,
however, turns into a disaster when Hulot breaks the lawn
sprinkler system, dousing all the guests in water. Only
Gérard and the Arpels' maid are amused.

Ultimately, M. Arpel decides to give Hulot a job in his own
company, hoping to add some stability to his brother-in-law's
life. Hulot, however, falls asleep at his station on the assembly line and allows a machine making plastic tubing to run
amuck. He tries to hide the misshapen tubing from M. Arpel
and that night is seen with Gérard and a group of friends,
dumping the plastic into the river. Hulot baby-sits for his
nephew while the Arpels dine out in celebration of their anni-
versary. When the Arpels return home, however, they find the
house in disarray, with Hulot sleeping on an upside-down sofa.

For M. Arpel, this is the last straw, and he arranges for
Hulot to get a job in another city. M. Arpel and Gérard take
Hulot to the airport. On their way home, a comic incident be-
falls M. Arpel. Rather than being annoyed, however, he is
amused, and a new relationship seems to blossom between father
and son. The influence of Hulot, thus, lives on.

Credits

Producer:	Fred Orain, Specta Films, Gray Film, Alter Films (Paris), and Film del Centauro (Rome)
Director:	Jacques Tati
Screenplay:	Jacques Tati with the collaboration of Jacques Lagrange and Jean L'Hote
Photography:	Jean Bourgoin
Set decoration:	Henri Schmitt
Music:	Frank Barcellini and Alains Romans
Sound:	Jacques Carrière
Editor:	Suzanne Baron
Assistant directors:	Henri Marquet and Pierre Etaix
Production director:	Bernard Maurice
Production adviser:	Fred Orain
Associate producers:	Louis Dolivet, Alain Térouanne
Cast:	Jacques Tati (M. Hulot), Jean-Pierre Zola (M. Arpel), Adrienne Servantie (Mme. Arpel), Alain Bécourt (the Arpels' son, Gérard), Lucien Frégis (M. Pichard), Dominique Marie (the Arpels' neighbor), Betty Schneider (the landlord's daughter), J. F. Martial (Walter), André Dino (the street sweeper), Max Martel (the drunkard), Yvonne Artaud (the Arpels' maid), Claude Badolle (the ragman), Nicolas Bataille (the workman), Régis Fontenay (the suspender salesman), Adélaide Danielli (Mme. Pichard), Denis Pêronne (Mlle. Février), Michel Goyot (the car salesman), Francomme (the painter), Dominique Derly (M. Arpel's secretary), Claire Roca (Mme. Arpel's friend), Jean Rêmoleux (client at the factory), Mancini (Italian salesman), René Lord, Nicole Regnault, Jean Meyet, Suzanne Franck, Leriot, Marguerite Grillières (citizens of Vieux Saint-Maur)
Locations:	Interiors filmed at La Victorine in Nice. Exteriors filmed at Créteil and Saint-Maur-des-Fossés
Running time:	110 minutes
Color process:	Eastmancolor

English version: Titled <u>My Uncle</u>, or <u>My Uncle, Mr. Hulot</u>

Note: The film received the following awards: Special Jury Prize, Cannes (1958); Prix de la Commission Superieure Technique Du Cinéma (1958); Medal of Gold from the Federazione Italiana del Circolo del Cinema (1958); Prix Belles de L'Association Française de la Critique Cinéma; Premier des Film Français de L'Année, Switzerland (1958); Special Jury Prize, Festival De Mar Del Plata (1958); Prix San Jorge, Spain (1958); Special Jury Prize, Czechoslovakia (1958); Gold Plaque, Festival of French Film, Rio De Janeiro (1958); Kunniakirja Award, Finland (1958); Golden Laurel Award, Edinburgh Film Festival (1958); Oscar for Best Foreign Film, Hollywood (1959); New York Film Critics Award for Best Foreign Film (1959).

10 PLAYTIME (1967)

Synopsis

The film begins at the Paris airport where people are arriving and departing on flights, and a variety of comic incidents are transpiring. An important dignitary arrives and is pursued by photographers; a lavatory attendant, changing towels, is mistaken for a nurse; a woman carries her dog in a red plaid piece of luggage. Among the people in the airport are a rather vocal group of American tourists and M. Hulot, who is seen scurrying by in the midst of the crowd. The tour group is met by a guide who whisks them into buses. Seeing the modern Parisian skyline and the huge parking lots, one tourist asks another, "Are you sure this is Paris, <u>France</u>?" Hulot also leaves the airport and is seen boarding a bus.

From this point on, the narrative traces the experiences of both Hulot and the tour group, whose activities continually overlap and intertwine. At first we follow Hulot, who has an appointment with a M. Giffard at a modern Parisian high-rise office building. Various gags ensue that are based on Hulot's problems navigating this glass-and-steel structure—with its mirrorlike walls, its automatic elevators, its escalators, and its mazelike series of office cubicles.

While searching for M. Giffard, Hulot wanders mistakenly into the office building next door in which a trade exposition is taking place. Here he again encounters the American tourists who have been brought there to sightsee by their guide. In particular, he notices a young woman tourist named Barbara, who seems rather disturbed and perplexed by the Paris she has found. In the trade exposition, the tourists witness demonstrations of such ridiculous products as "antique" garbage pails, doors that slam silently, and vacuum cleaners with headlights. Meanwhile, Hulot, in search of M. Giffard, runs into problems with two German salesmen and with ladies who mistake him for an employee.

As evening comes, the tourists are driven to their various hotels, and Hulot gets on a bus in the midst of a crowd. Characteristically, he holds on to a standing lamp base that someone is carrying instead of the bus support pole. Evening finds the tourists in the hotel preparing for their night out on the town at the elegant Royal Garden restaurant, which is opening that very evening. Hulot happens to pass the Royal Garden and stops to watch its frantic last-minute construction. There he runs into M. Giffard, the man he had sought earlier in the day. They go for a walk.

Meanwhile, the Royal Garden chaotically prepares for its opening, but much of the construction has not yet been completed. Paper is being rolled off the floor as guests arrive, and the coat-check girl is caught in the act of vacuuming. The neon sign on the restaurant marquee is still being installed and tiles stick to the waiters' feet. The architect runs around, madly taking notes on everything that needs to be repaired. Confusion reigns supreme in the kitchen as well, where the cook finds the pass-through too small to accommodate a tray.

In the midst of this chaos, the customers begin to arrive, among them, the American tourist group. As soon as they do, all sorts of problems arise: stair lights malfunction, waiters bring orders to the wrong tables, the air-conditioning system breaks down.

As the evening progresses, Hulot passes by the Royal Garden again on his walk with M. Giffard. He is eyed by the Royal Garden doorman who, it turns out, is an old army buddy. He invites Hulot in, but the latter refuses by closing the door. In the tug-of-war that ensues, Hulot breaks the glass front door. Henceforth, the doorman simply pretends there is a door by holding the doorknob in an appropriate place.

Hulot enters the restaurant. The situation within the Royal Garden rapidly deteriorates. When Hulot obliges a woman by reaching a flower for her on the wall, the entire ceiling collapses, causing a fiery explosion of light fixtures. Rather than spoiling the evening, the destruction of the stuffy restaurant decor seems to liberate it, and people begin to have fun. A group (including Hulot) form a kind of bistro in the corner of the room where they sing and dance.

As dawn comes, a group of people wander into Le Drugstore for breakfast. Hulot and Barbara stroll outside to a department store where Hulot intends to buy her a souvenir Paris scarf. As he does so, Barbara realizes that she must board her tour bus. She leaves and Hulot sends a surrogate to deliver the scarf.

As the tourist bus departs in the crowded traffic circle, the entire scene is transformed into a kind of fair. The bumper-to-bumper cars look like horses on a carousel; a cement mixer looks like an amusement park ride; a child on the street looks like a clown. The film ends at dusk, with Paris illuminated by the jewel-like lights of buildings, and traffic on the roads.

Credits

Producer:	Specta Films
Associate producer:	René Silvera
Director:	Jacques Tati
Screenplay:	Jacques Tati
Artistic collaborator:	Jacques Lagrange
English dialogue:	Art Buchwald
Photography:	Jean Badal and Andreas Winding
Art direction:	Eugène Roman
Music:	Francis Lemarque, David Stein (theme: "Take My Hand"), James Campbell (African themes)
Sound:	Jacques Maumont
Editor:	Gérard Pollicand
Production director:	Bernard Maurice
Cameramen:	Paul Rodier and Marcel Franchi
Cast:	Jacques Tati (M. Hulot), and, in order of appearance, female performers: Barbara Dennek (the young tourist), Jacqueline Lecomte (her friend), Valérie Camille (Mr. Lacs's secretary), France Rumilly (eyeglass saleswoman), France Delahalle (the client at the Strand), Laure Pailette, Colette Proust (the two women with the lamps), Erika Dentzler (Mme. Giffard), Yvette Ducreux (cloakroom attendant), Rita Maiden (M. Schultz's companion), Nicole Ray (the singer), Luce Bonifassy, Evy Cavallaro, Alice Field, Elaine Firmin-Didot, Ketty France, Nathalie Jam, Oliva Poli, Sophie Wennek (the clients of the Royal Garden); male performers: Jack Gauthier (the tour guide), Henri Piccoli (the important gentleman), Léon Doyen (the porter), Georges Montant (M. Giffard), John Abbey (Mr.

Lacs), Reinhart Kolldehoff (the German director), Grégory Katz (the German salesman), Marc Monjou (the false Hulot), Yves Barsacq (a friend), Tony Andal (the page boy at the Royal Garden), André Fouché (the manager of the Royal Garden), Georges Faye (the architect), Michel Fancini (the first maitre d'hotel at the Royal Garden), Billy Keans (Mr. Schulz), Bob Harley, Jacques Chauveau, Douglas Reard (the clients of the Royal Garden), François Viaur (the unlucky waiter), Gilbert Reeb (the girl-chasing waiter), Billy Bourbon (the barfly)

Location: The set for the film ("Tativille") was built at Saint-Maurice, outside of Paris.

Running time: 150 minutes in the original version. The film was cut by 15 minutes after its Parisian premiere. For American and British release, it was cut by approximately 30 minutes to 2 hours. American prints vary. Some have an introduction in which Tati appears to explain the film. Prints also vary in their inclusion of a scene in which Hulot peers into the windows of M. Giffard's apartment. Tati has said that the original version is the only one that he "believes in."

Technical process: Eastmancolor. Originally released in 70mm and stereophonic sound.

English version: Playtime

Note: The film won the following awards: Scandinavian Oscar (1968); Prix de L'Académie du Cinéma, Etoile de Cristal (1968); Danish Academy Award for the Best European Film of the Year (1969); Prix D'Argent at the Moscow Film Festival (1969); Best Film of the Year, Austria (1969); Kunniakirja Award, Finland (1969); Grand Prix de la Maison Internationale du Cinéma (1969).

11   TRAFIC (1971)

Synopsis

   In Trafic, Hulot is a designer at the Altra automobile

plant. The film begins as Hulot sneaks into the Altra factory
late, on the day that Altra sales people are readying cars for
exhibit at the annual automobile show in Amsterdam. It is decided that Hulot should supervise the trip to Holland. Also
slated for the journey are Marcel, a workman, some salesmen,
and Maria, one of the Altra publicity people.

The camping car is loaded on a truck which Hulot and Marcel
drive. Others set out in a station wagon, laden with false
logs on the luggage rack, to be used for a "rustic" exhibition
display. Maria follows in her sports car. Periodically, the
focus of the film switches to Amsterdam, where preparations
for the auto show are being made. Workmen have trouble deter-
mining which end of a Japanese car crate is up; announcements
on a public address system waft through the hall inaudibly.

When the narrative returns to Hulot and cohorts, we find
them stopped by the side of the road; their truck has run out
of gas. Hulot decides to walk ahead with a can in pursuit of
gas, but notices another man with an empty gas can walking in
the opposite direction. Hulot, therefore cuts across a field
to a small town. He fills up his can at a gas station and returns to the Altra truck.

The group sets out again, and we see a series of shots of
various other drivers, some of whom are listening to ridiculous
radio commercials, picking their noses, or stopping at "Antar"
gas stations to collect free gifts of absurd "historical" plas-
ter busts. On the road, Hulot stops at a strange garage,
filled with wrecks, and makes a call to Amsterdam, explaining
that he and his group will be late.

From this point on, the narrative chronicles the other ac-
cidents and mishaps that beset Hulot and delay his arrival.
Maria accidentally leads the truck across the border without
making the proper stop, and Holland police detain the Altra
party. In the police station, inspectors go over every inch
of the camping car, suspecting the presence of drugs. Their
inspection occasions a demonstration of the recreational vehicle's nonsensical accoutrements: a fender grill that can be
used for broiling steaks, a car horn that doubles as an electric razor, seat belts that are worn like suspenders.

While the Altra group is detained, the narrative periodically shifts to the automobile show which is already in progress.
Hundreds of salesmen simultaneously open and close car doors
and trunks for the eyes of potential customers; an exceedingly
frail old man has trouble extricating himself from a sports
car. Finally, the Altra group is released from the police
station and sets out again.

Shortly, however, they find themselves in the midst of a balletic, chain-reaction traffic accident, in which the prized camping car is dented. Thus, the are delayed yet again. They make their way to the home of a Dutch car mechanic who assures them that he will fix their car within a day. After more comic occurrences (one involving the mechanic's wife, and one a prank some neighborhood boys play on Maria's dog), the Altra group sets out again for the automobile show.

Finally, Hulot, Marcel, and Maria arrive in Amsterdam, only to find that the automobile show is already over. It was scheduled for the sixth of the month, which Maria mistook for the ninth. Blaming the fiasco on Hulot, the director fires him. The film closes with a comic montage sequence which establishes an equation between the personalities of cars and their drivers. In the final shot, Hulot and Maria are seen negotiating a traffic jam maze of bumper-to-bumper cars.

Credits

Producer:	Robert Dorfmann, Films Corona (Paris), Gibé Films, Oceania Films (Rome)
Director:	Jacques Tati
Screenplay:	Jacques Tati in collaboration with Jacques Lagrange
Photography:	Andreas Winding
Set decoration:	Adrien de Rooy
Music:	Charles Dumont
Editing:	Maurice Laumain and Sophie Tatischeff
Cameraman:	Marcel Weiss
Production manager:	Marcel Mossoti
Assistants:	Marie-France Siegler, Alain Payner, Roberto Giandala (with the participation of Bert Haanstra)
Cast:	Jacques Tati (M. Hulot), Maria Kimberly (Maria), Marcel Fravel (Marcel, a truck driver), Honoré Bostel (the director of Altra), François Maisongrosse (a buyer at Altra), Tony Kneppers (a Dutch garage owner).
Location:	Filmed in Holland
Running time:	96 minutes
Color process:	Eastmancolor
English version:	Traffic

Note: This film won the following awards: Fremio Nazionale Eur., Italy (1972); Outstanding Film of the Year, London Film Festival (1972); Kunniakirja Award, Finland (1972); Coupe Valdotaine D'Or, Italy (1973).

12   PARADE (1973)

Synopsis

"[Parade] is the story of a great festival in the course of
which Tati organizes an encounter between spectators, artists,
clowns, children and himself. In the course of this encounter,
adults and young people form a single enthusiastic mass, united
by the spectacle. From the beginning of the film, a little
girl and a little boy symbolize, in a single exchanged glance,
the joy of the entire ensemble, and, during the course of the
spectacle, which borders . . . on circus and music-hall, the
public participates directly, and Tati, as M. Loyal, leads and
animates the encounter.

The entrance of the public into the circus presents a series
of observations typical of Tati's art, such as the incredible
confusion which reigns in the cloak-room, or the woman, charged
with all the worries of the world, who finds herself in the
midst of hundreds of motorcycle helmets belonging to the spectators, or the scene in which a woman spectator, whose vision
is blocked, asks a young girl, seated in front of her, to take
off her helmet; the latter accedes courteously, but her hairdo,
liberated from the helmet, blocks the spectator's field of
vision even more . . .

The spectacle goes on before the eyes of the public and all
the symbols of modern life, which Tati rejects, are transformed
by him in the pure joy and harmony of the music hall. In the
course of the spectacle, Tati presents his great numbers: . . .
football, tennis of today and yester-year, the horse and rider,
fishing. Tati's numbers alternate with other exceptional
music-hall acts, of which the chief attraction is the sequence
with the mule, and the triumph of children over adults.

At the end of the film Tati puts the gigantic circus spectacle in the hands of the two children who appear at the beginning of the film, and, in the hall, empty of all spectators but
the parents, they realize, in their own manner, some colorful,
rhythmic numbers. The film ends on a night scene, in front of
the great circus; the lights go out, the wind carries off some
balloons . . ." (From the Cannes Film Festival program, 1974;
Museum of Modern Art, NYC Study Center Files; my translation)

Credits

Producer:	Gray-Film, Sveriges Radio and CEPEC
Director:	Jacques Tati
Screenplay:	Jacques Tati
Photography:	Jean Badal and Yunnar Fisher
Art direction:	François Bronett
Music:	Charles Dumont

Orchestration:	Armand Migiani; "Tax Free" by Jan Carlson
Sound:	Jean Neny
Editors:	Sophie Tatischeff, Per Carlesson, Siv Lundgren, Jonny Mair, Aline Fress
Production directors:	Louis Dolivet, Michel Chauvin
Executive producer:	Karl Haskel
Cameramen:	René Chabal, Jens Fisher, Bengt Nordwall
Cast:	Jacques Tati (M. Loyal), Karl Kossmayer and his mule, The Williams, The Veterans, The Sipoles, Norman and Ladd, Los Argentinos, Johnny Lonn, Bertilo, Jan Swahn, Bertil Berglund, Moniqa Sunnerberg, Pierre Bramma, Michèle Brabo, Pia Colombo, Hall
Running time:	83 minutes
Technical process:	Color

Note: Most of Parade was originally shot on videotape for a television show in Stockholm, Sweden. The film was shown on French television in 1973 and again at the Cannes Film Festival of 1974 out of competition. It has not been in commercial distribution in the United States and is, therefore, difficult to see. The film won the following award: Gold Medal in the Children's Film Competition at the Moscow Film Festival of 1975.

IV. Writings about Jaques Tati

1936

13   COLETTE. "Spectacles de Paris, Revue de L'A.B.C." Le
      Journal (28 June).
           Review of a mime performance by Tati in which Colette
      speaks of his art as entailing dance, sport, satire, and
      the tableau vivant. She compares Tati to a mythological
      centaur because of his ability to portray both "ball and
      racket, football and goal, horse and rider."

1949

*14   ANON. "Jour de fête." Ciné-Digest (July).
           Cited in Cauliez, entry 192, p. 189.

15   L'HERBIER, MARCEL. "Jour de fête du cinéma ou le miracle des
      bicyclettes." Combat (16 July).
           L'Herbier compares DeSica's The Bicycle Thief and Tati's
      Jour de fête, both of which were released in 1949. In addi-
      tion to their common use of the bicycle as a central prop,
      L'Herbier sees both films as unified by their style of rad-
      ical film realism, though the former assumes a tragic tone,
      and the latter, a comic tone.

16   MAXI. "Jour de fête." Variety 174 no. 11 (25 May):18.
           A review of the Paris premiere of Jour de fête which
      stresses its low-budget status and Tati's fine performance.
      The author calls the film a "big grosser" and a "natural
      for the foreign pix circuit."

17   VERDONE, MARIO. "Jour de fête." Bianco e Nero, no. 10, p. 87.
           A critical piece in which Verdone discusses the reasons
      for the late recognition of this film, and identifies
      "rhythm" as Tati's basic comic structure.

1950

1950

18 ESCANDE, JEAN-PIERRE. "Jour de fête." Fiche filmographique, no. 18. Paris: Institut Des Hautes Études Cinématographiques, 5 pp.

An in-depth analysis of the film. Part I gives extensive "documentation" (film credits) as well as some background information on Tati and coscenarist, René Wheeler. Part II summarizes the scenario and breaks it down into discrete segments. Part III deals with dramatic analysis. In this section, the author attempts to analyze the comic style of the film, which he sees as a cross between a "comedy of observation" and an American-style burlesque.

19 G.L. "Jour de fête." Monthly Film Bulletin 17, no. 196 (April-May):59.

A positive review of the film which remarks on such issues as its lack of plot, Tati's skill as a mime, and its experimentation with sound.

*20 KRIER, J. "Tati ne veut plus faire roue libre." L'Écran Français (15 November).

Cited in Cauliez, entry 192, p. 189.

21 QUÉVAL, JEAN. "Jour de fête." Sight and Sound 19, no. 4 (June):165-66.

A positive review of Jour de fête which concentrates on the plot but also provides some useful production information. Quéval notes the "thin narrative line" of the work and remarks that Tati, himself, "is the film." He also notes that the gags are reminiscent of the Mack Sennett shorts and states that Tati is the "only clown and comedian worthy of the great burlesque tradition, to be seen on the screen in recent years."

1952

22 ANON. "The Big Day (Jour de fête)." Variety 185, no. 11 (20 February):6.

A review of the film which opened on 19 February 1952 at the 55th Street Playhouse in New York City. The article quotes an earlier review of Jour de fête in Variety by "Maxi," written when the film opened in Paris in 1949 (see entry 16). At that time, "Maxi" had called the film's comic line "thin" but had predicted it would be an international success.

23   ANON. Review of Jour de fête. Time (31 March).
       A fairly positive review in which it is claimed that
     Tati has transplanted Mack Sennett's pratfalls to the French
     provinces. It calls the film a "tenuous little spoof-on-a-
     bicycle" which is "no weightier than a postcard."

                                1953

24   ANON. "Encore un fois Monsieur Hulot." Filmforum (July).
       A positive review of Les Vacances in which Tati is com-
     pared to Linder and Chaplin.

25   ANON. "Les Vacances." Bianco e Nero 14 (November):78-81.
       A review of the film which comments on its "structural
     simplicity and almost surreal naiveté." Among the stylistic
     elements mentioned are the mannequin-like characters who in-
     habit the film, Tati's minimal use of camera movement, his
     high-contrast photography, and the paucity of close shots.

*26 ANON. "Les Vacances." Télérama (Radio-Cinéma) (15 March).
       Cited in Agel, entry 62, p. 115.

*27 ANON. "Tati vous a-t-il fait rire." Télérama (Radio-Cinéma)
       (15 April).
       Cited in Agel, entry 62, p. 115.

28   ARNOUX, ALEXANDRE. "La Cinéma muet a-t-il existé?" La
       Parisienne (June):802-5.
       An article about Les Vacances in the context of its use
     of sound. Arnoux argues that there was never a "silent
     cinema," because of the standard use of music, sound ef-
     fects, narration, and titles. On the other hand, he argues
     that the best of cinema has always remained "silent" in
     terms of being unencumbered by too much dialogue. He,
     therefore, applauds the sound track of Les Vacances for its
     deluge of incomprehensible words.

29   AUREL, JEAN. "Vive Monsieur Hulot." La Parisienne (June):
       831-33.
       An article about Les Vacances which calls it the "newest,
     most comic film of the year." Aurel praises Tati's sound
     track and his original comic style which is not American,
     boulevard comedy, or burlesque. He talks with Tati, who
     speaks of his desire to shoot in color and of his opposition
     to the traditional film industry.

30   BAZIN, ANDRÉ. "Il successore di Max Linder." Cinema Nuovo,
       no. 12 (1 June):339-40.
       According to Bazin, Tati is the most important comic

1953

author since the Marx Brothers. Although Tati's comic
style can be compared to Mack Sennett's and Chaplin's,
Bazin finds considerable difference in their approach,
since Tati relies more on character than on situation for
comic effect.

31 _____. "Pas de scenario pour M. Hulot." Esprit (July):90-95.
One of the first major critical pieces written on Tati.
Bazin introduces many important analytical concepts concern-
ing the director's work--ideas that will form the basis of
critical writing on Tati for many years to come. Bazin be-
gins by placing Tati's work within a historical context.
He speaks of the fact that although comedy was born in
France with Max Linder, it died out with the ascendancy of
American comedy. He then discusses certain French comedians
who emerged during this "hiatus" (Fernandel and Raimu) as
well as the directors, Jacques and Pierre Prevert. For
Bazin, the release of Jour de fête in 1949 came as an unexpected surprise, carrying the promise of renewed life for
French comedy. Les Vacances, he finds a triumph: "It is
not only a question of the most important comic work of the
international cinema since the Marx Brothers and W. C.
Fields, but an event in the history of the sound cinema."
Bazin then goes on to discuss the aspects of Les Vacances
that he finds revolutionary: (1) the "unachieved" quality
of the Hulot persona; (2) the extraordinary temporality of
the film and its lack of traditional narrative structure;
(3) the film's sound track which caricatures sound; and
(4) the observational style of Tati's comedy. Reprinted:
Entry 203. Translated: Entry 340; Chapter VIII of the
present volume.

*32 _____. Review of Les Vacances. Liens (May).
Cited in Agel, entry 62, p. 115.

33 BONICELLI, VITTORIO. Review of Les Vacances. Tempo (Milan)
(5 November).
A positive review of Les Vacances that mentions Tati's
affinities with the spirit of childhood.

*34 CHEVALIER, J. "Tati renouvelle le comique." Image et Son,
no. 62 (April).
Cited in Cauliez, entry 192, p. 190.

35 DEHEURE, JACQUES. "Les Vacances." Fiche filmographique, no.
69. Paris: Institut Des Hautes Études Cinématographiques,
8 pp.
A detailed analysis of Les Vacances. Part I provides
credit and production information, biographic details, and

a short bibliography. Part II gives a plot summary and a
breakdown of the narrative into sequences. Part III analyzes editing and shot composition, sound, and decor. Finally, Part V discusses the work's thematic implications.
Deheure also points out important aspects of Tati's style:
his emphasis on the flow of time, his use of depth of field
and of the frame as "mask," and his long-take style, which
encourages spectator participation.

*36   De MONTIFERRAND, F. "Tati Hulot." Télérama (Radio-Cinéma)
        (15 November).
            Cited in Cauliez, entry 192, p. 190.

37   DONIOL-VALCROZE, JACQUES. Review of Les Vacances. France-
        Observateur (19 March).
            A review of Les Vacances which mentions the strange
        ambience of the film created through the sound track.
        Doniol-Valcroze sees the film as both "elliptical and docu-
        mentary."

38   LALOU, E. "Hulot je t'aime." Arts, no. 402 (13 March):4.
            A review of Les Vacances which sees it as a perfect syn-
        thesis between French comedy (where the gag was "invented")
        and American comedy (where the gag was "patented"). Lalou
        also defends the film against certain charges of plotless-
        ness.

39   MAURIAC, CLAUDE. Review of Les Vacances. Le Figaro
        Littéraire (4 April).
            A review of Les Vacances in which Mauriac calls attention
        to the innovative editing of the film. He also mentions the
        tone of satirical caricature and the aura of tragedy beneath
        the comedy.

40   MOSK. Review of Les Vacances. Variety 190, no. 8 (29 April).
            A positive review of the film which sees it, however, as
        less successful than Jour de fête. The reviewer mentions
        its characterization of various French "types," its minimal
        story line, and Tati's similarities to Mack Sennett.

41   PARMION, SERGE. "Enfin Tati revient." Cahiers du Cinéma,
        no. 22 (April):49-50.
            An article about Les Vacances and its long-awaited arri-
        val on the French film scene. Parmion is impressed by
        Tati's social satire, which transforms "a sinister, ordinary
        Trou-Sur-Mer into a harbor of grace." He also remarks on
        the slack narrative line which unifies the various episodes,
        and finds comparisons between Tati and such earlier masters
        of film comedy as Linder, Chaplin, and the Marx Brothers.

1953

42   P.H. "Les Vacances." Monthly Film Bulletin 21, no. 240:6-7.
       Credits, plot summary, and a review of Les Vacances.
     The reviewer is only "mildly amused" by Tati's comedy and
     conjectures that the director's "sense of timing is often
     at fault." Tati is praised, however, for his satire of
     seaside vacationers.

43   QUÉVAL, JEAN. "Les Vacances." Le Mercure de France (1 May):
       118-22.
       A mixed review of the film which finds the character of
     M. Hulot less memorable than his predecessor, François.
     Although he praises certain aspects of the film (its coun-
     terpoint of dialogue, its simultaneous centers of interest),
     Quéval complains about its lack of story line and conven-
     tional dramatic emphasis. Nevertheless, he concludes that
     Tati is the only contemporary French auteur "with a head
     for comedy."

*44   _____. "Le Type qui fonce." Télérama (Radio-Cinéma) (8 June).
       Cited in Cauliez, entry 192, p. 190.

45   SAUVY, ALFRED. "À propos de M. Hulot." Esprit (August):
       243-45.
       An article on Les Vacances which emphasizes the theme of
     the integration of the individual into a social milieu.
     Sauvy sees Hulot in a long line of literary and dramatic
     outsiders, like Kafka in The Castle or Charlot in Modern
     Times. Like Chaplin's tramp on the assembly line, Hulot is
     continually ejected by the vacation "machine" of the seaside
     resort. Sauvy ends by calling Tati a "genial primitive" and
     hoping that he, too, stays an outsider to the traditional
     film industry.

46   TALLENAY, JEAN-LOUIS. "Les Français n'ont-ils pas la tête
       comique?" In Sept ans de cinéma français, by Agel, H.;
       Barrot, J.-P.; Bazin, A.; Doniol-Valcroze, J.; Marion, D.;
       Quéval, J. Q.; and Tallenay, J.-L. Paris: Les Éditions du
       Cerf, pp. 52-58.
       Tallenay begins by bemoaning the fact that since the end
     of World War II, France has not produced any important comic
     films. He attributes this phenomenon to the paucity of com-
     ic talent in French scenarists, rather than to any lack of
     competent French comic performers. He then goes on to state
     that the only cause for optimism in this genre are the films
     of Noel-Noel and Jacques Tati. Tallenay mentions his anti-
     cipation of Tati's next film, Les Vacances, and ends the
     piece by stating that the dormant state of French comedy is
     particularly upsetting since France was the birthplace of
     silent comedy.

47   VILLARS, GILBERT. "Jacques Tati: Les Vacances." La Nouvelle
      Revue Française, no. 5 (May):923-24.
          A positive review of Les Vacances which calls Tati "one
      of the most original and assured" directors in French cin-
      ema. He praises Tati's use of sound, but remarks that his
      comedy is perhaps too subtle or delicate to satisfy most
      viewers.

                                1954

48   AMENGUAL, BARTHÉLÉMY. "L'Étrange Comique de Monsieur Tati."
      Cahiers du Cinéma, no. 32 (February):81-86.
          A critical piece on the early films of Tati and the
      first of a two-part article. Amengual claims that in Jour
      de fête and Les Vacances, Tati introduces a new type of
      cinematic comedy, one which blends traditional burlesque
      with a more realistic comedy of observation. He also dis-
      cusses the difference between the character of François in
      Jour de fête and Hulot in Les Vacances. The former is a
      more traditional comic type, inherently humorous. Hulot,
      however, derives his comic demeanor from his relations with
      other people and from their response to him.

49   _____. "L'Étrange Comique de Monsieur Tati/Part II." Cahiers
      du Cinéma, no. 34 (April):39-45.
          In this second part of a long critical piece, Amengual
      discusses the sense of abstraction in Tati's films that
      lurks beneath the surface realism. He feels that Tati ac-
      complishes this "by the suppression of almost anything ac-
      cidental which individualizes" objects. Rather he renders
      them like "catalogue figures, cut-out games, and coloring
      books." Amengual then goes on to speak of Tati's sound
      tracks, which he feels are revolutionary because they pre-
      sent sound from an "omniscient" point of view, rather than
      tied to the subjectivity of any character. In speaking of
      the lack of sound perspective in Les Vacances, he coins the
      term auditory cubism. He also discusses the sense of dis-
      tended temporality in Les Vacances and ends the article by
      examining the social critique in Tati's films.

*50   CARTA, J. "Le rugbyman du 7ᵉ Art." Temoignage chrétien
      (24 December).
          Cited in Cauliez, entry 192, p. 190.

51   COLLONE, HENRY. "Hulot-Berlu." Positif, no. 9 (December):
      10-12.
          An article about Les Vacances which sees it as confirming
      the promise of Tati's earlier film, Jour de fête. Collone

                                83

1954

sees the strength of the film in Tati's portrayal of the
quotidian figure of Hulot, who articulates a "contre-temps"
to the rhythm of the robot-vacationers. Collone ends by
stating that Tati's contribution to the cinema is in his
style of film observation.

52   FISHER, DAVID. "Les Vacances." Sight and Sound 23, no. 3
      (January–March):148.
          A generally favorable review of Les Vacances. Fisher
      discusses what he sees as the "charming" and effortless
      quality of Tati's films, characterizing them as not so much
      being made as "having happened." However, he finds the
      character of Hulot charmless and animal-like, and he com-
      pares him to "an amiable pipe-smoking grasshopper." Fisher
      stresses Tati's interest in the inanimate and mentions the
      gags involving the car and kayak. He closes the review by
      calling Tati's screen persona a true "eccentric" in the man-
      ner of W. C. Fields.

53   HOLL. Review of Mr. Hulot's Holiday. Variety 195, no. 3
      (23 June):6.
          An extremely positive review of the film which states
      that it recalls the best of silent comedy. The reviewer
      mentions Tati's comedy of situation and the film's universal
      appeal.

54   JEAN, RAYMOND. "Les Couleurs de la vie." Cahiers du Cinéma,
      no. 34 (April):46–48.
          An article inspired by Tati's Les Vacances, which dis-
      cusses the cinema's particular gift for rendering a sense
      of quotidian, daily existence. As Jean writes, "One of the
      most original possibilities of the cinema is to render per-
      ceptible to us quotidian banality without itself becoming
      banal." Jean contrasts this with the contemporary novel
      which he feels attempts less successfully to capture this
      theme. Jean feels that Tati's choice of the subject of va-
      cation in Les Vacances is particularly brilliant, since the
      holiday situation renders the theme of boredom and banality
      in its rarefied state. Jean makes an interesting comparison
      between Les Vacances and Vigo's À propos de Nice.

55   JOHNSON, M. ELIZABETH. "Mr. Hulot's Holiday." Films in
      Review 5, no. 7 (August–September):367.
          A review of Mr. Hulot's Holiday in which Johnson dis-
      cusses her mixed response to the film. Although she finds
      Tati's portrayal of all the "types" one finds at a French
      seaside resort admirable, and his satirical treatment of
      inanimate objects inventive, she has reservations concern-
      ing his performance style. She finds his pantomimic devices

1954

"too few and too little varied," stating that he often merely "bobs about like a slow-motion Jack-in-the-box." She also criticizes the film's mixture of mumbled dialogue and pantomimic silence. Nonetheless, she states that the film "has a lot of comedy to recommend it."

56   KNIGHT, ARTHUR. Review of Les Vacances. Saturday Review
      (19 June):30.
          A positive review which calls Les Vacances a "one man film." Knight remarks on the film's brilliant gags and its lack of conventional narrative line.

57   MORANDINI, MORANDO. "Il mimo Tati legge gli uomini." Cinema
      (Rome), no. 135 (10 June):333.
          In this interview, the filmmaker talks about his plans for Mon oncle and declares his preference for Les Vacances over Jour de fête, for DeSica ("the poet") over Rossellini ("too intellectual"), and for "reading" living experience rather than books and films.

58   PAINLEVÉ, JEAN. "Permanence de M. Hulot." Positif, no. 9
      (December):7-9.
          An article that discusses the current controversy over reactions to Les Vacances, and an impassioned defense of the film. Painlevé describes the French public as divided into two groups—those who like Les Vacances and those who do not. In opposition to the latter, Painlevé suggests forming "Hulot clubs," or "friends of Hulot" societies. In his defense of the film, Painlevé discusses Tati's act-ing skill and his interesting use of silence and an inaud-ible text—a quality that many proponents of "film-theatre" oppose. Painlevé also stresses Tati's "violation" of cer-tain laws of comedy. Rather than repeat a gag immediately, he choreographs gag repetition over the entire course of the film.

59   SPERI, PIETRO. "Estra e limiti di Tati." Cinema (Rome), no.
      134:305-7.
          A critical piece on Jour de fête and Les Vacances in which the author suggests that the actor, not the filmmaker, is the creator of the comic film and acknowledges Tati's originality in understanding this. Speri sees Tati's limi-tations in his lack of a definite style, which he feels be-trays the filmmaker's "dilettantism."

60   SUBIELA, MICHEL. "En regardent couler la grimauve." Positif,
      no. 9 (December):13-15.
          An article about Les Vacances which terms Tati's comedy "existential," and compares his film to works by such

1954

writers as Camus. Subiela talks of Les Vacances as being
a "testimony" to our times. He also mentions its revelation of "daily absurdity," as well as the "malaise of in-
communicability which characterizes human relations."
Subiela sees the film as populated with caricatured, stereo-
typed characters who fall into the categories of "the stupid
and false" or the "simple and tender." Hulot and his com-
patriots belong to the latter. Subiela sees the most ex-
istentially significant gag of the film as being that of
the sagging taffy, because it puts Hulot in the predicament
of not knowing if he should let it fall to the ground, catch
it, or let others intervene. As Subiela inquires, "Are we
very far from 'nauseau'?"

61   TATI, JACQUES. "Jacques Tati: Il y a erreur sur la personne."
      Cahiers du Cinéma, no. 42 (December):49.
           Tati responds to two questions concerning censorship that
      Cahier editors posed to important French directors: (1) If
      no worried censor existed to "safeguard good morals," what
      would we see in your films? (2) Have they already cut any
      erotic scenes from your films? Clearly, Tati finds these
      questions irrelevant to his cinematic concerns. He claims
      that without censorship we would see exactly what we do see
      in his films, and states that his main problems have been
      with distributors, not censors.

                              1955

62   AGEL, GENEVIÈVE. Hulot parmi nous. 7ᵉ Art. Paris: Éditions
      Du Cerf, 118 pp.
           The first book written on the films of Tati. The open-
      ing section summarizes Tati's music-hall career and dis-
      cusses his various sports mimes. A discussion of Jour de
      fête follows in which Agel concentrates on situating Tati's
      work in relation to the tradition of Clair, Chaplin, Linder,
      and Sennett. She introduces the concept of comic realism
      in relation to Jour de fête and demonstrates how that film
      prefigures Les Vacances. The second, and major, section of
      the book discusses Les Vacances in terms of several issues:
      Tati's peculiar sense of temporality, and his sense of com-
      edy based on realistic observation. She also discusses the
      manner in which Tati's humor is based on various kinds of
      chance, how certain gags arise from coincidence or misunder-
      standing. She next turns to an analysis of the character
      of M. Hulot and his relation to the realm of childhood.
      She ends with a chapter in which she links Tati to such
      literary and art historical figures as Cervantes, Rabelais,
      Gogol, Beckett, and Toulouse-Lautrec. The book contains a

1956

filmography and bibliography, as well as a list of sequences from Les Vacances.

63 ANON. "Jacques Tati." Unifrance Film Bulletin 34 (February-March).
     A discussion of the success of Les Vacances and Tati's current work on Mon oncle. Biographical information is also included.

*64 BAZIN, ANDRÉ. "Les Vacances." France-Observateur (8 September).
     Cited in Cauliez, entry 192, p. 189.

65 BUCHWALD, ART. "Jacques 'Hulot' Tati's American Spectacular." New York Herald Tribune (23 August):4.
     A short interview with Tati following his return to Paris from the United States where he appeared in an NBC television special. Tati complains to Buchwald that his producers wanted him to cut his sports mimes by some twenty-two seconds. Luckily, the show's producer, Max Liebman, interceded, and Tati was able to do the mimes in their original form.

66 CHARDÈRE, B. "Jacques Tati." Cinéma 55, no. 3 (January): 45-47.
     An interview with Tati in which he speaks on various issues: the basis of his comedy in observation; his love of the long-shot; his frustration with critics who fault his films for their lack of "dramatic structure"; the differences between the characters of François and M. Hulot.

67 MAYER, ANDREW. "The Art of Jacques Tati." Quarterly of Film, Radio and Television 10, no. 1 (Fall):19-23.
     A critical analysis of Les Vacances and of Tati's work in general.

1956

*68 ANON. "Jour de fête." Télérama (Radio-Cinéma) (9 September).
     Cited in Cauliez, entry 192, p. 190.

69 ANON. "Le Double Jeu/II: Les Metteurs en scène français." Cahiers du Cinéma 11, no. 66 (December):55.
     A short biographical sketch of Tati.

*70 ANON. "Les Vacances." Télérama (Radio-Cinéma) (21 October).
     Cited in Cauliez, entry 192, p. 190.

1956

71   GUTH, P. "J'ai vu Tati tourner son prochain film." Le Figaro
      Littéraire (29 September):4.
           An article written while observing Tati shoot on the set
      of Mon oncle. Guth discusses Tati's use of color and his
      employment of two locales: the Saint-Maur section of Paris
      and the Victorine Studios in Nice. Guth also speaks to
      Tati about his early background as an apprentice in his
      father's picture-framing shop and his formative years in
      the music hall and cinema.

72   KRYOU, ADO. "Tati et le monde extérieur." Cinéma 56
      (October-November).
           Kryou praises the work of Tati for its essential realism,
      which he finds atypical of most film comics and even of the
      so-called film realists. For Kryou, the latter present a
      synthetic "slice of life," whereas Tati presents "life it-
      self." Whereas other comics operate on the assumption that
      it is "me against the external world," Kryou sees Tati as
      proclaiming "me and the external world."

73   THÉVENOT, JEAN. "Pas de vacances pour M. Hulot." Les Lettres
      Françaises, no. 633 (23 August):1, 8.
           An article about Tati at work on Mon oncle after recover-
      ing from a serious automobile accident. Thévenot recounts
      the scenario and comments on Tati's sense of observation
      and careful preplanning of gags. Thévenot comments that
      Tati "has a horror of time, but mounts his gags with the
      precision of a clock-maker." He also comments on Tati's
      "democratic comedy," in which the spectator takes an active
      rather than a passive role.

74   TRUFFAUT, FRANÇOIS. "Connaissez-vous Mon oncle?" Arts, no.
      580 (8 August):1, 3.
           A conversation between Tati and Truffaut while the former
      is preparing Mon oncle, which begins shooting in several
      weeks. Tati discusses the film's scenario, its attack on
      the ultra-modern, and various offers he has had to play
      Hulot in other directors' films.

1957

75   ANON. "Make Them Laugh." Films and Filming 3, no. 11
      (August):15.
           An interview with Tati stressing the differences between
      his comic style and that of Chaplin. Illustrated.

76   ANON. "Soixante metteurs en scène français." Cahiers du
      Cinéma, no. 71 (May):63.

A short summary of Tati's work which declares him to be
a French "neo-realist filmmaker" and emphasizes the "strangeness" of his films. Biography and filmography are included.

*77 ANON. "Tati au travail." Ciné-Revue (8 February).
     Cited in Cauliez, entry 192, p. 189.

78 BEYLIE, CLAUDE. "Jacques Tati inconnu." Cinéma 57, no. 23:
    10-14.
        Beylie discusses the short films of Tati made in the
    1930s--works that both Tati and critics have tended to ig-
    nore. Among the films discussed are Gai Dimanche, On
    demande une brute, and Soigne ton gauche. Beylie provides
    capsule plot summaries and remarks on the relationship be-
    tween Tati's early films and his later work. He sees as
    primary in Tati's comedy his role as an athlete who dreams
    of conquering the world and is never discouraged by failure.
    Rather than showing force, Tati's athlete is "gallant and
    sweet," and it is from this reserve that his disappointments
    stem. Beylie concludes by calling Tati "one of the grandest
    embodiments of free man."

79 L'HOTE. "À Propos de Mon oncle." Cinéma 57, no. 119 (June):
    33.
        An article on Tati and the film Mon oncle.

80 MONOD, MARTINE. "Jacques Tati ou le passioné raissonable."
    Les Lettres Françaises, no. 693 (24 October):1, 5.
        An article about Mon oncle and an interview with Tati
    prior to the film's release. Monod reports that the film
    is a French-Italian coproduction and that it took eight
    months to shoot, three months to edit, and one to post-
    synchronize. Also discussed are the two sets for the film
    --one in Saint-Maur and the other at the Victorine Studios
    in Nice. Monod talks of Tati's use of nonprofessional ac-
    tors in the film and how six hundred people were auditioned
    for parts.

81 TRANCHANT, FRANÇOIS. "Dossier: Jacques Tati." Image et Son,
    no. 107 (December):15-17.
        A collage of statements by Tati and his critics on such
    topics as his music-hall background, the lack of plot in
    his films, his gag structure, and the realism of his comic
    style.

1958

82 ALPERT, HOLLIS. Review of My Uncle, Mr. Hulot. Saturday

1958

Review (15 November).
A fairly negative review in which Alpert criticizes Tati
for being "too serious," a quality which "prevents him from
making a wholly satisfactory comedy."

83   ANON. "Fiche filmographique #43. Jour de fête." Image et
       Son 114 (July):22.
       Documentation and analysis of Jour de fête.

84   ANON. "Fiche filmographique: Mon oncle." Image et Son, no.
       113 (June).
       Documentation and analysis of the film.

85   ANON. "Fiche filmographique: Mon oncle." Télécíné 75-76
       (June-July).
       Documentation and analysis of the film.

86   ANON. "For Variety: Automation, Insanity and War." Cue
       (8 November).
       An enthusiastic review of Mon oncle, which contains
       quotes from an interview with Tati in which he speaks of
       the follies of automation.

87   ANON. "Mon oncle." Arts, no. 651 (7 January):1.
       A photograph of Tati shooting Mon oncle and a notice of
       its upcoming release.

88   ANON. "Mon oncle." Cinéma 58 (June):28.
       An interview with Tati concerning Mon oncle.

*89   ANON. "Mon oncle." Fiches du Cinéma, no. 157 (1 June).
       Cited in Cauliez, entry 192, p. 188.

90   ANON. "My Uncle." Filmfacts (31 December):236-38.
       This article presents a synopsis of Mon oncle followed
       by excerpts from various reviews of the film.

91   ANON. Review of Mon oncle. New York Post (4 November).
       A brief review of Mon oncle.

92   ANON. Review of My Uncle. Time (1 December).
       A negative review of the film that criticizes Tati for
       not being "content to be merely a comedian," but rather at-
       tempting to load his films with social significance. The
       reviewer also finds the film too long and without "rhythmic
       respiration."

*93   ANON. "Tati parmi les comiques." Télérama (Radio-Cinéma)
       (26 October).
       Cited in Cauliez, entry 192, p. 190.

*94   BAZIN, ANDRÉ. "Mon oncle." L'Éducation Nationale (29 May).
        Cited in Cauliez, entry 192, p. 159.

95   BAZIN, ANDRÉ, and TRUFFAUT, FRANÇOIS. "Entretien avec Jacques
        Tati." Cahiers du Cinéma, no. 83 (May):2-20.
            An extensive interview with Tati. Among the issues dis-
        cussed are Tati's attempt to render a truthful style of
        comedy, his desire to make a film without Hulot, his rela-
        tionship to Chaplin and Keaton, his use of color and fixed
        camera position, and his emphasis on audience participation.
        The interview is followed by a short biographical sketch, a
        filmography, and brief bibliography.

96   BECKLEY, PAUL V. "Mon Oncle Made in Two Versions." New York
        Herald Tribune (16 November).
            Beckley corrects a formerly published statement that
        Mon oncle was shown in New York City in both a French lan-
        guage and an English-dubbed version. He says, rather, that
        an English version was shot by Tati simultaneously with the
        French version. (A letter from Tati to this effect accom-
        panies the article.) Beckley also points out various ef-
        fects of Tati's use of English--its monotone delivery and
        its continual mixture with French. He recommends that view-
        ers see both versions to catch all comic nuances.

97   BEYLIE, CLAUDE. "Le pesanteur et la grâce." Cahiers du
        Cinéma, no. 84 (June):50-52.
            An article on Mon oncle which praises Tati's use of quo-
        tidian detail and observation in his comedy. Beylie remarks
        that the character of Hulot has lost its aura of caricature
        and, in Mon oncle, is more like "a dreamer in a nightmare
        world." He remarks on Tati's tendency to efface himself
        and speaks of his desire to make a film without Hulot.
        Beylie also discusses Tati's status as a sports mime and
        talks of his athletic skills and the "arabesque" of his
        body. He ends by saying that he admires Tati for his mul-
        tiple roles as architect, sportsman, poet, acrobat, and
        dancer.

98   BUCHWALD, ART. "Art Buchwald in Paris: Brigitte and Tati."
        New York Herald Tribune (16 October).
            In this article, following the Paris opening of Mon
        oncle, Buchwald claims that the film has made more money
        than any other French film of 1958. He then sketches a
        part-realistic, part-mocking interview with Tati who is
        about to leave for the United States in order to publicize
        his film. Tati complains about the way Americans are al-
        ways asking him about Brigitte Bardot, at which point
        Buchwald mischievously launches into a series of questions
        concerning the sex goddess.

1958

99   CARRIÈRE, JEAN-CLAUDE. <u>Les Vacances de Monsieur Hulot</u>. Paris:
      Éditions Robert Laffont. 198 pp.
          A novel based on Tati's film. Illustrations are by
      Pierre Étaix who worked with Tati on <u>Mon oncle</u>.

100   _____. <u>Mon oncle</u>. Paris: Éditions Robert Laffont.
          A novel based on Tati's film. Illustrations are by
      Pierre Etaix who was an assistant director to Tati on <u>Mon
      oncle</u>.

101   CASAMAYOR, L. "Une Histoire d'enfant." <u>Esprit</u> (November):
      669-70.
          An article on <u>Mon oncle</u> which discusses it as thematical-
      ly centering on the subject of childhood. Casamayor sees
      it as a film about the Arpel son--ignored by his unloving
      parents and nurtured by his uncle Hulot. Casamayor defends
      the film against certain claims by other critics that it
      attacks urbanism and the concept of work. Ultimately,
      Casamayor sees the film as less satirical than poetic.

102   CAULIEZ, A. J. "<u>Mon oncle</u>." <u>L'Age Nouveau</u>, no. 103 (July):
      133-36.
          An in-depth discussion of the film which cites Tati as
      one of the three major "artisans" responsible for a renais-
      sance in French cinema--the others being Bresson and
      Rouquier. What he finds special about Tati's style is his
      preference for "phenomenological realism," and the study of
      "critical moments of human reality" as opposed to grand
      drama. Cauliez compares Hulot to Charlot and finds the
      former unique in his lack of centrality to the film's narra-
      tive. He also speaks of Tati's use of color (to make the
      image "readable") and of his employment of the static long-
      take. He concludes by discussing Tati's politics and says,
      "<u>Mon oncle</u> is to progress what pacifist films are to total
      warfare."

103   CHARENSOL, G. "<u>Mon oncle</u>." <u>Les Nouvelles Littéraires</u>, no.
      1603 (22 May):10.
          A review of <u>Mon oncle</u> which compares Tati to Chaplin and
      states that it confirms Tati's ability to "impose his vision
      on life." He claims, as well, that Hulot incarnates the in-
      dividual "who refuses to allow himself to be incorporated
      into the masses." He speaks also of Tati's Bergsonian repe-
      titions, his use of sound, his employment of color, and his
      subtly deployed gags. He calls <u>Mon oncle</u> a work of "strange
      poetry."

104   COOK, ALTON. "Tati Tickles Funny Bone." <u>New York World
      Telegram and Sun</u> (4 November):6.

1958

A very positive review of Mon oncle in which the author says that Tati's "rapier of satire is hilariously keener than ever."

105   CROWTHER, BOSLEY. "Slapstick Comedy: Jacques Tati in a Classic Vein in Film My Uncle." New York Times (9 November).
       A positive review of the film which compares Tati to such slapstick heroes as Chaplin, Keaton, and Lloyd. Crowther finds Tati "preserving a type of humor that is almost lost on the screen."

106   DONIOL-VALCROZE, JACQUES. "Tati sur les pattes de l'oiseau." Cahiers du Cinéma, no. 82 (April):1-3.
       A discussion of Mon oncle. The author points out an apparent lack of story line in the film, but goes on to note that the film charts a progression in the relationship between M. Arpel and his son as mediated by Hulot. Doniol-Valcroze describes the two opposing universes posited by the film: that of the factory and ultra-modern Arpel home, and that of Hulot's old quarter.

107   FAYARD, JEAN. "Le cinéma." Revue de Paris (July):163-64.
       A very favorable review of Mon oncle that claims that the criticism against the film (for its length, its gag repetition, its lack of narrative line) are all ill-founded. Fayard sees the film as a successful "battle between two universes." In the sections concerning the Arpel home, Fayard finds the film most like Chaplin's Modern Times, and in the sequences concerning the old quarter, more like the work of René Clair. He finds the lack of a story line balanced out by the high degree of poetry in the film.

108   GANNE, GILBERT. "Tati sans caméra." Les Nouvelles Littéraires, no. 1605 (5 June):8.
       An interview with Tati in which he speaks of his views on Paris architecture, parking problems, and so on. Tati also discusses his formation of Spectafilm in 1956, and his work method.

109   GERALD, YVONNE. Review of My Uncle. Films in Review 10, no. 10 (December):587-90.
       An illustrated article on Tati's work which traces his career through Mon oncle. Gerald first relates certain biographic material on Tati: his French/Russian heritage, his family's picture-framing business, and so on. She then describes Tati's acting role in Sylvie and the Phantom. Gerald next discusses The Big Day (Jour de fête), stressing its use of slapstick comedy and its fascination with the bicycle as machine. In examining Mr. Hulot's Holiday,

1958

> Gerald sees a continued interest in inanimate objects dis-
> played in Tati's use of Hulot's old car. The remaining
> part of the article centers on a review of <u>Mon oncle</u> which
> has been recently released. Gerald stresses Tati's minimal
> use of dialogue, which she sees as permitting the director
> an international audience. She also terms the character of
> Hulot "a situational, not a personality comedian." In gen-
> eral, Gerald's review is favorable.

110   GILBERT, JUSTIN. "New 'Hulot' Film at Guild, Baronet." <u>New
      York Mirror</u> (4 November).
>   A positive review of <u>Mon oncle</u> in which Tati is compared
> to Chaplin. The reviewer does, however, complain of Tati's
> "tendency to ramble."

111   GUYONNET, RENÉ. "Le XI festival de Cannes." <u>Les Temps
      Modernes</u>, no. 150–51 (August–September).
>   A report from the Cannes Film Festival which bemoans the
> fact that the Golden Palm went to Kalatazov's <u>The Cranes
> Are Flying</u> and not <u>Mon oncle</u>. Guyonnet speculates that the
> Golden Palm was not awarded to the latter because a French
> film won the short-film category. Guyonnet praises the film
> for its use of fragmentary dialogue and for its "clear real-
> ism"--a style which "turns its back" on burlesque. Guyonnet
> compares the film with <u>Modern Times</u> and finds Tati interested
> less in the alienation of labor as in the dehumanization of
> contemporary decor and the loss of human contact. Ultimate-
> ly, however, Guyonnet criticizes the film for what he feels
> is a doltish nostalgia for the "good old times." He seems
> to argue that Tati should have placed more emphasis on a
> critique of the petit-bourgeois class than on the failings
> of contemporary design. Nonetheless, he argues that Tati
> has produced the best "social psychoanalysis" of France to
> have emerged in the last few years.

112   HALE, WANDA. "Guild and Baronet Show New Tati Film." <u>New
      York Daily News</u> (4 November).
>   A generally favorable review of <u>Mon oncle</u> which was
> showing in two versions in New York theaters: English-
> dubbed and subtitled.

113   HELLEUR, STAN. "Tati Takes a Tumble in Latest Rib-Tickler."
      <u>Toronto Globe and Mail</u> (20 December).
>   A negative review which claims that <u>Mon oncle</u> is "slop-
> pily put together" and that its attack on modernism is not
> funny.

114   MARSH, W. WARD. "Laughs Galore Fill 'Hulot' Film." <u>Cleveland
      Plain Dealer</u> (25 December).

A lukewarm review of Mon oncle which finds Tati less
than satisfactory as a comic performer. The reviewer wonders "what Fernandel would have done with this Hulot."

115   MARTINI, STELIO. "Sospetto per il Signor Hulot." Cinema
      Nuovo (Milan), no. 135 (September–October):107.
          A critical piece concerning Tati's sense of humor, based
      on an interview with the filmmaker. In discussing Les
      Vacances and Mon oncle, Martini identifies Tati's central
      interest as the observation of people's "automatic" behavior.
      He suggests that Tati's lack of ideological concern prevents
      him from posing an alternative to people's "standard behav-
      ior," and may eventually lead to an impoverishment of Tati's
      original critical position.

116   MEKAS, JONAS. Review of Mon oncle. Village Voice 4, no. 3
      (12 November):6.
          A review of Mon oncle which is discussed along with two
      other films. Mekas sees Mon oncle as an instance of inde-
      pendent cinema, the "uncorrupt, unprofessional film." He
      calls Tati "an amateur at heart, working outside the con-
      ventions of film acting and film 'art.'"

117   MILLER, DON. "Mon oncle." Films in Review (December):587.
          A favorable review of the film which claims it "really
      comes to grip with the technology of the modern world" and
      contains some of the "funniest bits of business seen this
      year."

118   MOSK. Review of Mon oncle. Variety 210, no. 12 (21 May):16.
          A generally positive review which finds the film "some-
      what long," but displaying "inventiveness, gags, warmth and
      a poetic approach to satire." The reviewer also mentions
      Tati's creative use of sound.

119   NASON, RICHARD W. "M. Tati in Praise of Innocence and Smiles."
      New York Times (2 November).
          An article on Tati on the eve of the New York City pre-
      miere of Mon oncle. It contains various quotes from an in-
      terview with Tati.

120   PELSWICK, ROSE. "Tati Spoofs Modern Age in Fine Style." New
      York Journal American (4 November):10.
          A positive review of Mon oncle which calls the film "an
      entertaining spoof on this mechanized age" and calls Tati
      a "talented satirist."

121   ROSS, DON. "Tati's 'Mr. Hulot' On Screen Again." New York
      Herald Tribune (2 November).

1958

> An article on Tati on the eve of the New York premiere
> of <u>Mon oncle</u>. It contains various quotes from an interview
> with Tati.

122 SADOUL, GEORGES. Review of <u>Mon oncle</u>. <u>Les Lettres Françaises</u>
(15 May).
> A review of <u>Mon oncle</u> in which Sadoul finds the trait of
> "modesty" at the heart of Tati's work. There is sexual mod-
> esty in Tati's refusal to show Hulot's bedroom. And Sadoul
> also finds modesty in Tati's technique--his refusal to "un-
> derline" a gag or to exploit an object until all its comic
> possibilities have been tapped.

123 SAUVY, ALFRED. "Charles Chaplin et Jacques Tati devant le
problème social." <u>Cahiers de la République</u>, no. 15
(September–October).
> An article about the social perspectives of Chaplin ver-
> sus Tati. In discussing Chaplin, Sauvy makes the point
> that his films are "devoid of class spirit." He also char-
> acterizes the figure of the Tramp as a "bourgeois manqué"
> whose costume signifies his aspirations toward the upper
> middle class. He also says that although some have mistaken
> <u>Modern Times</u> for a critique of capitalism, it is really only
> an attack on the machine itself. Turning to Tati (and in
> particular to <u>Mon oncle</u>), Sauvy makes the point that his
> work portrays two "societies" rather than two classes--that
> of the modern suburb and that of the old section of Paris.
> Furthermore, he feels that both are portrayed unrealistical-
> ly. The people in the old section seem perpetually on vaca-
> tion. The people in the modern society, on the other hand,
> perpetually spend their time complicating their existence
> with technology. All class struggle is absent. Sauvy re-
> fers to the film as high bourgeois propaganda, but realizes
> that Tati is ostensibly apolitical and clearly does not in-
> tend it as such. Sauvy then launches into a discussion of
> the Tramp versus Hulot, and finds the latter a singular
> comic figure because of his refusal to claim the status of
> victim--the typical position of the clown. Sauvy ends the
> piece by contrasting the biographies of Chaplin and Tati:
> the former from the working-class ranks, and the latter
> from the Russian aristocracy and French bourgeoisie. Iron-
> ically, he notes, Tati (the middle-class director) has had
> more problems gaining acceptance in film circles than
> Chaplin, ("the boy of the people"). Though Sauvy notes
> Tati's rebellious stance against the traditional film indus-
> try, he remarks that this hardly makes him a revolutionary.
> Sauvy concludes by noting that Tati is at a turning point
> in his career when he must make some difficult decisions
> concerning his relation to his public and his position on
> social issues.

1958

124 _____. "En jouant avec Tati." L'Express, no. 362 (22 May):25.
An article on Tati (by one of his former rugby mates),
which reminisces about his early mime improvisations. Sauvy
mentions one mime involving two Frenchmen crossing the
Atlantic en route to the United States, and another, satirical of radio. He wonders if France will realize that it
possesses the greatest living comic and accord Tati his due
place.

125 SLOCUM, BILL. "Americans Are Nuts But Nice, Tati Says." New
York Mirror (28 October).
A series of quotes by Tati upon his visit to the United
States to publicize Mon oncle. He speaks disparagingly of
American television and of how the bankers control film
production in both the United States and France.

126 TATI, JACQUES. "Jacques Tati raconte son nouveau film Mon
oncle." Arts, no. 663 (26 March):6.
Tati discusses his early years performing in the music
hall as well as his short films of the 1930s. He also mentions a major car accident in 1955 which held up his work
on Mon oncle until 1956. He speaks of the film as a contrast of two locales, and says that he was fortunately able
to make it with "complete artistic liberty."

127 THIRER, IRENE. "Movie Spotlight." New York Post (3 November).
A profile of Tati in which he speaks of his dislike for
television.

128 VINCENT, DENIS. "Mon oncle." L'Express, no. 361 (15 May):19.
An article on Mon oncle which considers it from a political point of view. Vincent warns that if bureaucrats do not
forbid their employees to see it, they may find their of-
fices deserted and their workers in revolt on the green
grass. Though he compares the film to Modern Times and À
nous la liberté, he finds that Tati has gone further in
terms of social commentary. Whereas Chaplin was concerned
with the effects of mechanization on workers, he sees Tati's
concern as alienation. Although he denies the film any real
"social signification," he says its portrayal of the Arpels
is that of bourgeois France. He concludes by stating that
one can discern Tati's Russian heritage in Mon oncle because the film is more reminiscent of Chekov than of Chaplin
or Feydeau.

129 VIVET, JEAN-PIERRE. Review of Mon oncle. L'Express, no. 361
(15 May).
A review from Cannes in which Vivet calls the film a
"merited and incontestable success." He praises the film

1958

for its abstract quality, its use of long-shots, its employment of amateur actors, and its use of sound. He finds the
film similar in effect to what Bresson has done in a dramatic mode.

130 WEALES, GERALD. "Movies: Jacques Tati and the Tyranny of
     Things." Reporter (27 November).
       A review of Mon oncle which calls the film "a comedy
     that has serious things to say about the mechanization and
     sterilization of society." Weales also discusses Tati's
     body language and compares him to Buster Keaton.

131 WEINBERG, HERMAN. "Mon oncle." Film Quarterly 12, no. 2
     (Winter):49-51.
       An illustrated review of Mon oncle in which Weinberg
     compares Tati to René Clair and Charlie Chaplin, though he
     finds him a lesser artist. Nonetheless he rates Tati "above
     all other comedians functioning in the world today."
     Weinberg discusses Tati's comic style, noting that he is
     not so much a classic mime as "frozen-faced," in the tradi-
     tion of Keaton. He also remarks that after only two films,
     the character of Hulot has "already become as recognizable
     . . . as the little tramp of Chaplin . . . and as lovable."
     Weinberg goes on to discuss Tati's satirization of Danish
     modern furniture and push-button gadgets. He then summar-
     izes the plot of the film, commenting on various gags.

1959

132 ANON. "French Comic Says U.S. Forgets How to Laugh." New
     York Herald Tribune (26 April):7.
       Tati discusses his conception of film humor, which he
     sees tied to the visual scene and not to jokes or puns.

133 ANON. "French Funnyman Tati Pays Embassy Visit." Post Times
     and Herald (13 December).
       An article reporting Tati's trip to Washington, D.C.,
     accompanied by a photograph of Tati with Mme. Alphand,
     wife of the French ambassador.

134 ANON. "Jacques Tati Overwhelmed on Visit to Film Capital."
     Newark Evening News (15 April).
       Tati speaks of the artificiality of Hollywood. He
     states, "The place seems so unreal, even the shops with
     their glittering facades appear to be only movie sets."

*135 ANON. "Mon oncle." Télérama (Radio-Cinéma) (25 October).
       Cited in Cauliez, entry 192, p. 190.

136   ANON. Review of <u>Mon oncle</u>. <u>Observer</u> (London) (11 October).
       A short positive review of the film.

137   ANON. "Tati découvre Les États-Unis." <u>Arts</u>, no. 720
       (29 April).
            An article concerning Tati's recent trip to the United
       States to receive an Oscar for <u>Mon oncle</u>.

138   BAKER, PETER. Review of <u>Mon oncle</u>. <u>Films and Filming</u> 5, no.
       11 (23 August):23.
            A generally favorable review of <u>Mon oncle</u> which states
       that "at a time when original screen comedy is almost non-
       existent, this is a gem not to be missed." Baker compares
       Tati to Chaplin, finding the former's concern with technique
       more intense. He does, however, fault Tati for his social-
       satirical emphasis, which he finds not always the greatest
       source of comedy.

139   B.D. "<u>Mon oncle</u>." <u>Monthly Film Bulletin</u> 25/26, no. 307:102.
            Credits, synopsis, and review of the film. The reviewer
       praises the film and situates it within the tradition of
       Chaplin and Clair. Cited are Tati's subdued use of color
       to create an "ideal world" and his use of amateur performers.

*140   GAUMONT, L. "Mon oncle revient d'Amérique." <u>La Cinématographie</u>
       <u>Française</u> (20 June).
            Cited in Cauliez, entry 192, p. 189.

141   HOUSTON, PENELOPE. "Conscience and Comedy." <u>Sight and Sound</u>
       28, no. 3-4 (Summer-Autumn):161-63.
            Houston discusses <u>Mon oncle</u> which she finds Tati's most
       substantial film. She mentions the character of Hulot and
       his "resistance" to human contact, as well as Tati's edit-
       ing and disregard for conventional film pacing.

142   JEANNE, RENÉ, and FORD, CHARLES. <u>Le Cinéma français</u>. Vol. 5.
       Paris: Éditions Robert Laffont, pp. 100-102.
            An encyclopedia entry on the career of Tati.

143   LE JEUNE, C. A. "M. Hulot's Return." <u>Observer</u> (London)
       (28 June).
            A favorable review which compares <u>Mon oncle</u> to <u>À nous la</u>
       <u>liberté</u> and <u>Modern Times</u>.

144   LOUIS, THÉODORE. <u>Jacques Tati</u>. Les Grandes Createurs du
       cinéma, no. 26-27. Brussels: Club de cinéma, 27 pp.
            A monograph on the films of Tati, from <u>Jour de fête</u>
       through <u>Mon oncle</u>. After a brief discussion of Tati's back-
       ground as a mime, Louis examines <u>Jour de fête</u> but dismisses

1959

it as theatrical and lacking in cinematographic qualities.
He nevertheless executes an in-depth analysis of the film
concentrating on Tati's relation to objects, and his curious
blending of the qualities of dreamer and mathematician.
Louis then examines Les Vacances, which he finds not only
successful but "a step in the history of cinema." He calls
Tati "a painter of boredom" and discusses how the film is
"obsessed with emptiness." He then grapples with the issue
of Tati's relation to realism. Louis also discusses Tati's
sense of time, but is most interesting in his analysis of
the director's sense of space. He notes the supreme importance of decor, and remarks on Tati's use of montage and
varied camera angles. Finally, Louis analyzes Mon oncle,
which he finds radical in its extreme stylization and its
use of color as a mode of signification. However, he ultimately finds Mon oncle lacking because of its abstraction
and its minimization of Hulot.

145 V.S. "Mio Zio." Cinema Nuovo 12, no. 137:60.
A review of Mon oncle in which the author identifies as
the central theme of the film the juxtaposition of two
(opposed) human conditions. One is represented by the
super-civilized bourgeois family and the other by the old-
fashioned, but genuine, "popular" community. According to
the author, Mon oncle's only flaw is the central character
of M. Hulot who fails to bridge the gap between the film's
two worlds.

1961

146 ANON. "Jacques Tati." In Current Biography. Edited by
Charles Moritz. New York: H. W. Wilson.
One of the most complete biographical sketches of Tati's
life.

147 MARCABRU, PIERRE. "Jacques Tati contre l'ironie française."
Arts (8 March).
Marcabru applauds the work of Tati who he feels has re-
sumed the tradition of French comedy. He notes Tati's precise preparation of gags, and compares Tati's creative in-
dependence to that of Bresson.

1962

148 ANON. "Les Vacances." Filmforum, no. 15:497.
An analysis of the film.

149   BASSOTTO, CAMILO. "Le Vacanze di Mr. Hulot." Cineforum, no.
       15 (May):497-512.
           A long critical piece on Tati in which the author ana-
       lyzes Tati's ideas about the nature of the comic character,
       the script of Les Vacances, its style, Tati's acting, and
       the film's dialogue, as well as sound and montage techni-
       ques. Bassotto concludes that the naivete and spontaneity
       of Tati's art helps us to rediscover novelty in familiar
       things, places, and people.

150   CAULIEZ, ARMAND J. Jacques Tati. Cinéma d'aujourd'hui.
       Paris: Éditions Seghers.
           This book, surveying Tati's films through Mon oncle, was
       later reissued in a second edition in 1968. See entry 192
       for complete annotation.

151   MARTAIN, GILLES. "Les Vacances." Arts, no. 858 (28 February):
       3.
           A rave review of Les Vacances which calls it "a classic
       of the cinema" and a "neo-realist masterpiece." Martain
       stresses the theme of boredom in the film and comments that,
       by contrast, the film leaves to the spectator's "imagination
       a certain role."

152   STRICK, PHILLIP. "Jour de fête." Films and Filming 8, no. 8
       (May):19-52.
           A plot summary and evaluation of Tati's film as well as
       a source of background information on its production. The
       critical response to the film is also summarized. Informa-
       tion is provided on Tati's earlier films: Oscar, champion
       de tennis, On demande une brute, and so on. Essentially,
       Strick sees the role of Hulot in Jour de fête as one of in-
       fusing "nonconformism into a conservative society."

1963

153   MITRY, JEAN. "Jacques Tati." In Dictionnaire du cinéma.
       Paris: Librarie Larousse, pp. 147, 252, 267.
           Mitry presents information on Tati under headings of
       Tati, Les Vacances, Mon oncle, and Jour de fête.

1964

154   ANON. "Jacques Tati Claims Novel New Film Tint Process."
       Variety (18 November).
           A report that Titi has discovered a process called
       Scopochrome by which he can turn black-and-white pictures

1964

into color. He hopes to release a group of old American
slapstick comedies reworked in this method, as well as his
own Jour de fête.

155   ANON. "Tati and Rohauer Buy Educational Films, 1,000 Shorties,
        60 Sennetts." Variety (16 September).
            A report of Tati and Rohauer's purchase of Educational
        Films, a collection of works from 1920 through 1940. The
        article also states that Tati and Rohauer have negotiated
        a partnership with Specta Films (Paris) for the global re-
        issue of many films. Tati, Bernard Maurice, and René Silvera
        will re-edit and update the films.

1965

156   ANON. "Journey to Tativille." Sight and Sound (August):162.
            An article about the extraordinary set for Playtime de-
        signed by Eugène Roman and located in Saint-Maurice.

157   ANON. "Voyage à Tativille." Cinéma, no. 99 (September-
        October):16-22.
            A description of a visit to Tativille, the elaborate set
        for Playtime which Tati had built outside of Paris. The
        author discusses Tati's reason for not shooting on location
        or in a studio and describes various activities that took
        place on the set. Tati is then interviewed. Among the
        topics discussed are his financial problems, his original
        title for the film (Recreation), the themes of his films,
        and his use of wide-screen format.

1966

158   ARMES, ROY. "Jacques Tati." In French Cinema from 1946.
        New Jersey: A. S. Barnes, pp. 145-58.
            A section on Tati in a history of postwar French film.
        The Tati section is later expanded and published separately
        in 1979. See entry 207 for annotation.

159   EYLES, ALLEN. "Les Vacances." Films and Filming 12, no. 5
        (February):51-52.
            A discussion of Les Vacances.

160   LENNON, PETER. "M. Hulot Recruits Army Wives." New York
        Times (13 March).
            Tati talks about his casting of American army wives as
        tourists in Playtime. He also speaks of hiring the lead
        character, Barbara, who, in real life, was a mother's helper
        working down the street from where Tati lived.

1967

161 NATTA, ENZO. "Tativille: Incontro con Jacques Tati."
     Cineforum, no. 54 (April):299-303.
         An interview with Tati during the filming of Playtime.
     Natta discusses with Tati such issues as his title for the
     film, his attitude toward contemporary architecture, his
     financial difficulties, and his reasons for shooting so few
     films.

                              1967

162 ANON. Film lexicon degli autori e delle opere. Vol. 7. Rome:
     Centro Sperimentale di Cinematografia, pp. 78-80.
         A biographical and critical summary of Tati's career,
     with filmography and bibliography.

163 ANON. "Playtime." Dossiers Art et Essai, no. 37 (28 December):
     39.
         An article containing Tati's filmography, certain produc-
     tion statistics regarding Playtime, credits for the film,
     and a summary of its scenario and various stills. Quotes
     by Tati about the film are included, as well as statements
     about Tati by André Bazin, Georges Sadoul, Pierre Marcabru,
     and Jean Cocteau.

164 ANON. "Playtime." [Pressbook.] Paris: Dessins de Cabu.
         A pressbook containing an introductory sketch of Tati's
     career by Henry Rabine, a discussion of the construction of
     the extraordinary set for the film, credits, and so on.

165 ANON. Review of Playtime. Paris-Match (30 December).
         A positive short review, placing Tati in the tradition
     of Keaton, and citing his strong sense of aesthetics and
     observation. The article does, however, mention certain
     "slow" sections.

166 BORY, JEAN-LOUIS. "L'Esprit de finesse." Le Nouvel
     Observateur, no. 163 (27 December).
         In this review of Playtime, Bory speaks particularly of
     Tati's "finesse"--the subtle quality of his humor. He notes
     Tati's lack of emphasis on auditory and visual gags, and the
     need for the spectator to respond to the film with great in-
     telligence. As he states, Tati is one of the few directors
     "not to take his public for a conglomerate of idiots." Bory
     talks of Tati's films as requiring an "agility of the eye"
     from the spectator, since he juxtaposes several gags within
     the frame. He also remarks on Tati's unfailing sense of
     realistic detail and observation. Bory concludes by saying
     that Tati's films make demands on the spectator's eye, ear,

1967

> intelligence, and heart--all of which participate in com-
> prehending the comedy.

167 CAPENDAC, M. "'L'arche de Noé'de Tati." Les Lettres
Françaises (27 December).
A review of Playtime that calls Tati the greatest comic
director since Linder. Capendac praises the quality of the
imagery and the use of 70mm format, and sees the thematics
of the film as a continuation of Mon oncle.

168 CHALON, J. "Avec Playtime, son 'come back,' Tati a-t-il
realisé son 'hit et demi'?" Le Figaro Littéraire
(11 December).
An interview with Tati on the occasion of the opening of
Playtime. Tati talks of his three-year preparation for the
film and his disappointment in having had to destroy the
set. "I wanted," he remarks, "to make this city a gift to
the young filmmakers." Tati speaks of himself as an artisan
like his father. He also states that, given his Russian
heritage, he would like to make a Russian-style film.

169 CHARENSOL, G., and GILLES, JACOB. "Cher Tati." Les Nouvelles
Littéraires, no. 2103 (21 December):14.
A mixed review of Playtime which calls the film "a large
visual poem." The reviewers do, however, find the film too
long and criticize the director's use of nonprofessional
actors.

170 CHAUVET, LOUIS. "Playtime." Le Figaro (18 December).
A positive review of the film which sees it as a
"Kafkaesque" comedy which mocks the age of glass, automation, and so on. Chauvet finds Tati's comedy more satirical
than that of the "philosophers of the absurd."

171 CHAZAL, ROBERT. "Playtime: Le chef d'oeuvre du rire."
France-Soir (19 December).
A rave review of Playtime which calls it "the greatest
French comic film" and ranks it as a privileged work in the
history of film comedy--along with those of Linder, Keaton,
and Chaplin. Chazal sees as the major theme the opposition
of nature versus technology, a notion he finds summarized
in the images of sky and skyscraper in the first few moments
of the film.

172 DAUSSOIS, GUY. "Playtime: un chef d'oeuvre d'ironie
souriante." Le Populaire de Paris (23 December).
A positive review of Playtime which calls Tati a "smiling
ironist." Daussois sees the film as divided into a satirical section and a section focusing on the comedy of manners.

He claims that we emerge from the film "lighter and more human."

173   De BARONCELLI, JEAN. "Playtime de Jacques Tati." Le Monde
      (22 December).
         A generally favorable review of the film in which De
      Baroncelli calls Playtime an "insane wager" and applauds
      Tati for taking risks. After talking about the construction
      of Tativille, he concentrates on the dual strains of laughter
      and poetry within the film. He mentions that because of
      public reaction, Tati will cut Playtime by twenty minutes.

174   GARSON, CLAUDE. "Playtime." Aurore (18 December).
         A mixed review of Playtime which finds the film suffering
      from a lack of proper cutting. He also finds Tati's project
      a bit hermetic. He writes that Tati has been "the master,
      then the prisoner. He has shut himself in his work and has
      been amazed by it."

175   GIROUD, FRANÇOISE. "Tati tout amorti." L'Express
      (25 December):35.
         A negative review of Playtime which praises Tati's effort
      and personal financial risk, but faults the film on its the-
      matic perspective. Giroud finds the satirical level of
      Playtime least successful and cites the apolitical Royal
      Garden sequence as the most effective. She also faults the
      film for its length, citing Chaplin as a comic director who
      knew when to end his films. Finally, she finds Tati's so-
      cial commentary banal, saying that he is "two revolutions
      late." She notes that our parents were shocked by six-story
      buildings which now seem quaint (as their parents were
      shocked by the railroad). Rather than seeing the objects
      Tati cites as "scandalous symbols of our scandalous civili-
      zation," she finds them only "convenient servants, and noth-
      ing more."

176   LACHIZE, SAMUEL. "Monsieur Hulot c'est notre Gulliver."
      L'Humanité (20 December).
         A review of Playtime which compares Hulot to Gulliver
      and Tati's satire to that of Swift. Lachize sees Tati's
      major theme as that of the contemporary failure of communi-
      cation, symbolized by the glass walls which surround and
      separate people.

177   LENOIR, THOMAS. "Tati et le temps des loisirs." L'Express
      (30 January):30-32.
         An interview with Tati in which he discusses the produc-
      tion of Playtime, his need for 70mm format, his construction
      of Tativille, and his slow and meticulous work pace. He

compares his situation to Chaplin and reminds the inter-
viewers that it took two years to shoot <u>The Gold Rush</u>.

178   MICHEL, JACQUELINE. "<u>Playtime</u>." <u>Télé 7 Jours</u> (30 December).
      A positive review of the film which sees Tati in the
      tradition of Chaplin, Keaton, and Linder. Michel sees
      <u>Playtime</u> as a comedy of the absurd, whose major themes are
      the uniformity and conformity of modern life.

179   MOHRT, MICHEL. "L'Anti-moderne." <u>Carrefour</u> (27 December).
      A positive review which finds <u>Playtime</u> Tati's unquali-
      fied masterpiece and a work in the tradition of Chaplin's
      <u>Modern Times</u>. The reviewer finds the second half of the
      film more successful than the first, and criticizes its
      slowness of pace and its repetition of certain gags.

180   MOSK. Review of <u>Playtime</u>. <u>Variety</u> 249, no. 6 (27 December):7.
      A very positive review of the film which says that Tati's
      ten-year hiatus from the cinema was well worth the wait.
      The reviewer says that Tati "has assimilated the greats but
      is an individual comic talent who builds meticulous gags
      founded on a gentle, anarchic individualism."

181   MOURLET, MICHEL. "Les confidences de M. Hulot." <u>Les
      Nouvelles Littéraires</u>, no. 2104 (28 December):14.
      A conversation with Tati in which he discusses his slow
      pace of work which he credits to the desire not to repeat
      himself. He also talks about his music-hall background,
      his refusal of various television series, and his advice
      to young filmmakers.

182   _____. "Tati on pas Tati." <u>Les Nouvelles Littéraires</u>, no.
      2100 (30 November):16.
      A visit to "Tati-City" (the set for <u>Playtime</u>) and an
      interview with Tati. Mourlet discusses the various statis-
      tics of the set's construction—the amount of concrete,
      plaster, and workers involved in the five-month effort.
      He also mentions how various buildings were mounted on
      rails so that they could be moved around at will.

183   PELLENQ, PAULETTE. "Sur <u>Playtime</u>." <u>L'Humanité Dimanche</u>
      (24 December).
      A positive review of the film which calls it one of the
      best films currently in Paris. Pellenq defends <u>Playtime</u>
      against unfavorable comparisons with Godard's <u>Two or Three
      Things</u> . . . , or Antonioni's <u>The Red Desert</u>. She says
      that it is inappropriate to view Tati as making a "defini-
      tive work on modern life." She particularly admires the
      film's dense sound track and deployment of simultaneous

gags. She feels that the film is the opposite of "cinema opium" because of the critical demands it makes on the viewer.

184 RENDU, MARCEL. "Tati et les temps modernes." Temoignage Chrétien (28 December).

An extended review and critique of Playtime. Rendu emphasizes what he sees as the apoliticism of the film, which he finds the proper stance of comedy. He contrasts Tati's ridicule of societal clichés to Godard's criticism of economic systems. Rendu also discusses the theme of voyeurism and exhibitionism in the film which he sees articulated in the set of glass houses. Ultimately, he sees Playtime as restoring for us a sense of curiosity in the details of daily life.

1968

185 A. J. "Playtime est bien accuelli à Londres par le public et la critique." Le Monde (17 July):12.

An article reporting the critical and public success of Playtime in its London exhibition.

186 ANON. "Playtime: Le Nouveau Film de Jacques Tati." Cinéma International, no. 77:761.

A short interview with Tati on Playtime, accompanied by several stills. One in particular is important since it is excerpted from the section of Playtime that was cut in the American-release version.

*187 ANON. Review of Playtime. Jeune Cinema 29 (March):31.

Cited in British Film Institute card catalogue.

188 ANON. "Tati." Cahiers du Cinéma, no. 199 (March):8-20.

An extensive interview with Tati concerning Playtime. It is, as well, an homage to Tati by the editors of Cahiers and a statement of critical respect for a film that had been generally misunderstood. Tati speaks in great detail on the following topics: the construction of the set for Playtime (Tativille); his use of 70mm format; his interest in de-emphasizing the Hulot character; his employment of a scenario; his attitude toward contemporary architecture; and his use of color, as well as his mode of gag construction. He also provides useful information concerning the cuts that his distributors forced him to make in Playtime, Mon oncle and Les Vacances. The interview is followed by a series of critical pieces on Tati by Jean-André Fieschi, Noel Burch, Paul-Louis Martin, and Jean Badal, as well as by a detailed filmography.

1968

189 BADAL, JEAN. "La Cathédràle de verre." <u>Cahiers du Cinéma</u>, no. 199 (March):28.
 A short critical piece in which Badal speaks of having watched Tati direct <u>Playtime</u> on the elaborate set he had constructed. Badal likens Tati's role as supervisor of the mise-en-scène to a choreographer or an orchestra conductor. Badal speaks particularly of how Tati often rehearsed a shot for three or four days before shooting, demonstrating actions to the performers and seeking a precise timing. Badal speaks as well about Tati's propensity for long-shots and of his use of color.

190 B.D. "<u>Playtime</u>." <u>Monthly Film Bulletin</u> 35, no. 415 (August):113–14.
 A negative review of <u>Playtime</u> which criticizes the film for its "shapelessness and repetition." Full credits are included.

191 BURCH, NOEL. "Notes sur la forme chez Tati." <u>Cahiers du Cinéma</u>, no. 199 (March):26–27.
 Burch begins by claiming that <u>Playtime</u> is Tati's second masterpiece and that it confirms the reputation he acquired some fourteen years earlier with <u>Les Vacances</u> and lost, to some degree, with the "failure" of <u>Mon oncle</u>. Furthermore, Burch feels that <u>Playtime</u> assures Tati a status as one of the greatest directors in the history of cinema. What Burch finds extraordinary about <u>Playtime</u> is its lack of a narrative pretext, and its complex gag construction which attains "a formal unity across a discontinuity of discourse." Thus Burch speaks of how gags are introduced in one sequence, completed in another, developed in a third, and refused in a fourth. Burch also emphasizes the "respiratory" quality of <u>Playtime</u>'s structure, which he feels is a result of the alternation of "strong" and "weak" moments. He also notes the evolution of gags from sequential construction in the opening Orly scene to simultaneous construction in the Royal Garden sequence. Finally, he points out how the Royal Garden sequence works as a microcosmic version of the film's overall structure.

192 CAULIEZ, ARMAND J. <u>Jacques Tati</u>. Cinéma d'aujourd'hui, Paris: Éditions Seghers, 186 pp.
 One of the most comprehensive works on Tati to date. It is the second edition of the 1962 text, updated to include a discussion of <u>Playtime</u>. In the first section, Cauliez gives a brief biographical sketch of Tati's career, one of the most complete biographies available. In the second chapter, he provides a concise overview of Tati's comic style, emphasizing his brand of documentary realism.

Chapter three provides a discussion of Tati's early films, stressing Mon oncle. Chapter four attempts a theoretical discussion of comedy and endeavors to categorize certain gag structures in Tati's films. Chapter five deals with the narrative structure of Tati's films, and chapter six is an examination of Playtime. The rest of the book provides various kinds of documentation: a selection of important quotes extracted from interviews with Tati; excerpts from scenarios for the films; selections of critical writings on Tati; and a complete filmography and bibliography of texts on Tati in French.

193   EYLES, ALLEN. "Playtime." Films and Filming 15, no. 1 (October):43-44.
      A favorable review of Playtime which also includes full credits. Eyles finds Tati's concern with urban life in Playtime a continuation of his interests in Mon oncle and even Jour de fête. He discusses certain gags based on the eclipse of quaint Parisian life: the lone flower seller, the monuments reflected in glass doors. Eyles discusses the character of Hulot and sees his function as primarily "to provide a line of continuity between scenes." Though Eyles finds the film's message "hardly new," he states that it is Tati's imaginative approach to the subject which makes Playtime "so richly rewarding." Eyles also notes the use of long-shots in Playtime and ends his review by remarking on the fact that the film was cut for British release. Unlike other critics, he suspects that this may have helped the film and saved it from "becoming over-extended."

194   FIESCHI, JEAN-ANDRÉ. "Le Carrefour Tati." Cahiers du Cinéma, no. 199 (March):24-26.
      Fieschi discusses Playtime in terms of its being a revolutionary and modernist work of cinema. Fieschi emphasizes various aspects of the film: Tati's creation of "a world" for the film through elaborate sets, and his "multiplication of characters" by generalizing the action from Hulot to others. Fieschi particularly stresses the overall structure of Playtime and claims that Tati has invented a new genre of comedy in which humor lies not in individual shots or gags but in the overall structure and the "invisible thread" that unites all narrative elements.

195   HART, DENIS. "How Jacques Tati Made the English Laugh." Daily Telegraph (2 August).
      A descriptive piece concerning Tati's career and an interview with him during the editing of Playtime. Tati gives some brief biographical information, speaks of comedy in general, and talks of his technique of casting Playtime.

1968

196   HOUSTON, PENELOPE. "Playtime." Sight and Sound 37, no. 4
       (Autumn):205.
            A review of Playtime which finds fault with the film for
       its trite message. Houston also finds "too little" to
       laugh at in the famous Royal Garden sequence.

197   MARTIN, MARCEL. "Playtime: Mon Oncle à Metropolis." Cinéma,
       no. 123 (February):99-101.
            A negative review of Playtime which criticizes the film
       for its distended structure and its lack of true satirical
       bite. Martin claims that comedy necessitates a philosophy,
       a situation, and a comic character--all of which Playtime
       lacks.

198   MARTIN, PAUL-LOUIS. "D'Un Tati l'autre." Cahiers du Cinéma,
       no. 199 (March):27-28.
            Martin's primary emphasis is on the relationship between
       Tati's four major feature films: Jour de fête, Les Vacances,
       Mon oncle, and Playtime. Martin feels that their trajectory
       is linear, and that he can discuss certain themes diachron-
       ically. He first discusses the evolution of the Tati per-
       sona from François in Jour de fête (who had a precise rela-
       tionship to the world) to Hulot in Playtime (who merely
       "exists"). He next examines the Tati character's relation
       to work, from François, the postman, in Jour de fête (who
       had a particular vocation) to Hulot in Playtime (who has
       some vague relation to business). He then discusses the
       status of nature in Tati's films and posits a movement from
       the natural, rural world of Jour de fête to the industrial,
       urban decor of Playtime. Finally, he discusses Tati's at-
       titude toward Americans in his films, as well as the evolu-
       tion of the role of objects in his work.

199   MAURIAC, CLAUDE. "Playtime." Le Figaro Littéraire
       (1 Jaunary).
            A positive review of the film that discusses its possi-
       bilities for American release. Mauriac mentions that the
       film has been cut by fifteen minutes since he first saw it,
       which he regrets. He speaks of the film's difficulty and
       of its simultaneous deployment of visual gags. He praises
       Tati's "negation and disarticulation of language," which
       he feels may have originated in Jour de fête for technical/
       financial reasons. He ends the piece by calling the film a
       "pure masterpiece" and Tati a "genius in its pure state."

200   SGUINZI, STEFANO. "Playtime." Cineforum, no. 75 (May):327-43.
            An in-depth article on Playtime, including "script" and
       critical analysis. After briefly discussing Tati's earlier
       films, Sguinzi examines various issues concerning Playtime:

its technical sophistication, the character of Hulot, Tati's
vision of Paris, and his attitude toward modern culture. In
terms of the latter, Sguinzi argues that Playtime is Tati's
reflection on contemporary life and on humanity's inability
to find a place in a consumeristic culture. According to
Sguinzi, in Playtime Tati denies the validity of prophesies
about people's automatism and depersonalization. Rather,
he sees them transcended by the value of the individual and
by poetry.

1969

201 ANON. "Directors of the Year: #5/Jacques Tati." In
     International Film Guide 1969. Edited by Peter Cowie.
     London: Tantivy Press, pp. 25-27.
        A brief discussion of the career of Tati on the occasion
     of his having been chosen a Director of the Year by the
     International Film Guide of 1969. After reviewing his
     earlier works, the article claims that Playtime is the first
     "international film--the first to switch between French,
     English and German with complete familiarity and success."
     The article closes with a filmography.

202 ANON. "Tati in Mood to Comic for U.S." Variety (29 January).
        An article reporting that after the financial disaster
     of Playtime (on which Tati spent $2 million), the director
     is considering making a film in the United States.

203 BAZIN, ANDRÉ. "M. Hulot et le temps." In Qu-est-ce que le
     cinéma? Ontologie et langage, vol. 1. Paris: Éditions
     du Cerf, pp. 109-15.
        Reprint of entry 31; translated: Entry 340; Chapter VIII
     of the present volume.

204 WOODSIDE, HAROLD G. "Tati Speaks." Take One 2, no. 6
     (July-August):6-8.
        An article occasioned by Tati's appearance in November
     at the National Film Theatre in London. Woodside describes
     certain aspects of that event: Tati's mimes, his use of
     film clips, and his lecture to the audience. The article
     also excerpts some quotes from an interview with Tati. He
     speaks particularly of his interest in color, his concep-
     tion of sound, his attitude toward modern architecture, and
     his emphasis on observation as a source of comedy.

1970

1970

205   ANON. "Jacques Tati." In Who's Who in the World. 1st Ed.,
      1971–1972. Chicago: Marquis Who's Who, p. 891.
          A brief biographical sketch of Tati, as well as a film-
      ography and list of awards he has received.

206   ARMES, ROY. "The Comic Art of Jacques Tati." Screen 2, no. 1
      (Fall):68–81.
          A revised version of the Tati section of Armes's French
      Cinema Since 1946 (entries 158 and 207), which pays more
      attention to Playtime. Armes provides an interesting read-
      ing of Tati's claim that Playtime is "an open window," re-
      lating it to the use of glass in the film. Armes also cri-
      ticizes the popular French position that Tati's work is
      related to Italian neo-realism.

207   _____. "Jacques Tati." In French Cinema from 1946. New
      Jersey: A. S. Barnes & Co., pp. 145–58.
          Revised version of entry 158. Armes's discussion of
      Tati constitutes one section of his survey of postwar
      French film directors. He classifies Tati under the heading
      of "Innovators and Independents." The first term refers to
      Armes's belief in Tati's highly original comic style; the
      second refers to the director's insistence on producing
      films outside the traditional commercial film system. Armes
      provides a general introduction to Tati's work from Jour de
      fête through Playtime. He includes some biographical in-
      formation and plot summaries, and makes certain critical
      points about the films. He also quotes from several inter-
      views with Tati to corroborate his own remarks. In general,
      Armes stresses Tati's emphasis on observation and ascribes
      to it the basis of his comic style. The book contains a
      filmography and a partial bibliography.

208   HALLIWELL, LESLIE. "Jacques Tati." In The Filmgoers
      Companion. 3d ed. New York: Hill & Wang, p. 938.
          A short biographical sketch of Tati and a list of his
      major films and awards.

1971

209   ANON. Review of Trafic. Cinemonde, no. 1851 (April):35.
          An article on the production circumstances of Trafic.

210   ANON. "Tati dans le trafic Parisien." Le Figaro (27 April).
          An article about Tati in Parisian traffic, accompanied
      by photographs.

1971

211 ANON. "Trafic de Jacques Tati." Le Monde (20 April).
     A positive review that says that after a four-year ab-
     sence, Tati has returned with a substantial work. The re-
     viewer finds Trafic "modest of ambition and budget" as
     compared to Playtime and displaying a stronger narrative
     thread. Tati's mixture of poetry and observation is men-
     tioned.

212 BAUDRY, PEIRRE. "Sur le réalisme." Cahiers du Cinéma, no. 31
     (August-September):35-41.
     A major critical piece on Tati which discusses the rela-
     tion of Tati's work to realism. This is a central issue
     because much of the earlier literature on Tati had centered
     around characterizing his work as comic "neo-realism."
     Baudry rejects this. He talks of various levels of fiction
     in the work of Tati: fantastic fiction (like Trafic's ab-
     surd camping car) and more subtle fiction. Also discussed
     are certain reflexive elements in Tati's work, and the way
     the films make the viewer conscious of their fictionality.
     Baudry also claims that every sound and image that appears
     in Trafic is there to create a certain meaning; thus, he
     introduces the notion of Tati as a "master of signs."

213 BILLARD, PIERRE. "Trafic de Jacques Tati." L'Express
     (19 April).
     A review of the film which finds it not as comic as Les
     Vacances and not as "heavy" as Playtime, but similar to Mon
     oncle. The reviewer also remarks that there is only one
     print of Trafic playing in Paris, a sign that Tati shuns
     the assembly line of cinema. Also discussed are Tati's use
     of a minimal narrative line and his comedy of observation.
     Billard does, however, criticize Tati's social commentary
     as less barbed than Chaplin's, and accuses him of a nostal-
     gic attempt to recapture past times. He also faults Tati
     for making his clowns so inhumane and asks him to give Hulot
     a "soul."

214 BURNETT, OCTAVE. "Fiche filmographique #553: Trafic."
     Télécine, no. 173 (October-November):17-23.
     An in-depth structural analysis of Trafic. The article
     begins with a listing of credits and a summary of the major
     sequences of the film. Then Burnett discusses the scenario
     for Trafic and notes that it reveals very little about the
     film. The same script might might, in fact, have functioned
     for a dramatic rather than a comic film. Burnett asks the
     question of why Trafic is, nonetheless, so unique and dis-
     tinctive. He then focuses his attention on the remarkable
     posters for the film in the Paris theater in which Trafic
     opened. He notes that in one poster, the word trafic was

1971

designed out of roadway graphics, and in another, a mirror on which the word <u>trafic</u> was inscribed reflected the real Parisian traffic outside. Burnett remarks that these posters may lead one to expect a film that is a reflection of reality, an assumption that proves wrong. Burnett goes on to discuss the structure of the film which he sees as centered on the camping car as "hero." Furthermore, Burnett sees the whimsical camping car as representing "fantasy" or "desire," as opposed to the laws of normality. He then analyzes the film's mise-en-scène, rhythm, dialogue, sound effects, music, montage, and acting style. Among the points discussed are Tati's slow comic style, his minimal use of dialogue, and the relation of his editing to the gag structure. In the next section, Burnett discusses the character of Hulot whom he sees as a "silhouette," or "shadow"-- an "extraterrestrial being." In the final section of the piece, Burnett opposes <u>Trafic</u> to Godard's <u>Weekend</u> and claims that the former is not a film of social criticism but a work of moral and poetic orientation.

215   CHAUVET, LOUIS. "M. Hulot et son <u>Trafic</u>." <u>Le Figaro</u> (17 April).
A positive review of the film which applauds its poetic atmosphere and "out-of-this-world" feeling. Chauvet particularly likes the opening auto-route sequence, and the subsequent accident montage.

216   COHN, BERNARD. "<u>Trafic</u>." <u>Positif</u>, no. 131 (October):58-60.
A positive review of <u>Trafic</u> in which Cohn emphasizes Tati's use of space, which he finds articulated with "stunning mastery." He also calls the film an "absurd ballet."

217   COMUZIO, ERMANNO. "Monsieur Hulot ne caos del traffico." <u>Cineforum</u>, no. 108 (October-November):41-52.
A long critical piece on <u>Trafic</u> in which Comuzio analyzes Tati's use of the automobile syndrome as an analogy for contemporary ways of looking at life. Comuzio concludes that Tati's comic vein consists of his ability to observe and to understand through observation.

218   EYLES, ALLEN. "<u>Traffic</u>." <u>Focus on Film</u>, no. 8 (December).
A short favorable review of <u>Trafic</u> with credits, biography, and filmography.

219   FLEURY, MONIQUE. "<u>Trafic</u>." <u>France-Soir</u> (19 April).
A positive review which states that the film allows Frenchmen to laugh at themselves; it also applauds Tati's poetic tone.

220 GILLIATT, PENELOPE. "The Current Cinema: Jacques Tati."
     New Yorker (28 August):58-61.
          An impressionistic piece on the career of Tati and the
     persona of Hulot, occasioned by the revival of Mon oncle.
     Gilliatt also discusses Mon oncle in some depth.

221 HAUSTRATE, GASTON. "Trafic: Du retard à l'allumage." Cinéma,
     no. 158 (July-August):131-32.
          A mixed review of Trafic with credits. Haustrate criti-
     cizes the slow pace and repetitiveness of the film, but
     praises certain "inspired" sequences--like the collective
     traffic accident. He also chides Tati for not going beyond
     a certain nostalgic tone in his work.

222 LOUBIÈRE, PIERRE. "Trafic." Télécine, no. 169 (May).
          A positive review of the film which finds it thematically
     relevant to Tati's earlier work. Also discussed is the pre-
     dominance of sound over image in the film. Loubière also
     mentions, in passing, François Truffaut's homage to Hulot
     in Domicile Conjugal.

223 MOSK. "Trafic." Variety (5 May).
          A positive review of the film at its Cannes exhibition.
     The reviewer claims that Tati is "probably still the most
     consummate one-man comic filmmaker practicing today."

224 ROSENBAUM, JONATHAN. "Paris Journal." Film Comment 7, no. 3
     (Fall):2, 4, 6.
          A review of Trafic which finds the film disappointing in
     relation to Playtime, Tati's masterpiece. Rosenbaum feels
     that Trafic regresses in its mode of comic construction.
     Whereas Playtime proposes freedom and participation to the
     spectator, Trafic represents rather "a prosaic string of
     bead-like gags." Rosenbaum, however, is more upset with
     the public's preference for Trafic over Playtime than he
     is with the failures of the former film itself.

225 _____. "Paris Journal." Film Comment 7, no. 4 (Winter):2, 4,
     6.
          A critical piece on Tati stressing Playtime. Rosenbaum
     begins, however, by making points about Tati's use of music
     in earlier films, as well as the complex audiovisual gag
     structure in Les Vacances. He then turns to an analysis of
     Playtime, noting the multiple points of interest and the
     spectator's attendant freedom of choice. Rosenbaum also
     discusses the division of the work into two parts: the
     first, in which the decor controls the people; and the sec-
     ond, in which the characters triumph over the decor.

1971

226   SARRUTE, CLAUDE. "Tati: Étonnez-vous!" Le Monde (15 April).
        An article about Tati on the eve of the release of Trafic.
        Sarrute visits him at his office and, in writing a profile
        of the director, defends his status as an artisan and a
        filmmaker who believes in making demands on the spectator.

1972

227   ANDREWS, NIGEL. "Traffic." Sight and Sound 41, no. 1
        (Winter):51-52.
        A negative review of the film which finds it "a fitful
        and disappointing successor to Playtime." It faults the
        film for its exclusive reliance on one-shot gags and for
        its paucity of extended jokes. It mentions that Trafic was
        originally a joint project with Dutch filmmaker, Bert
        Haanstra, who at some point terminated the collaboration.

228   ANON. "Traffic." Filmfacts 15, no. 24:653-55.
        A synopsis of the film, with excerpts from reviews by
        Roger Greenspun, Stanley Kauffmann, Andrew Sarris, Roger
        Ebert, Jay Cocks, Kathleen Carroll, and others.

229   CANBY, VINCENT. "Tati's Terrific Traffic." New York Times
        (16 December).
        A very favorable review of Trafic in which Canby dis-
        cusses the Hulot persona. He finds him not as "lovable" as
        in earlier films and less easy to identify with than Chaplin
        or Keaton. Rather, as Canby puts it, Hulot "exists as a
        kind of fixed point in a view finder with which we are able
        to put the rest of the world in focus."

230   CARROLL, KATHLEEN. "M. Hulot Is a Loser in the Modern World."
        Sunday News (26 November):28.
        A brief interview with Tati during his stay in New York
        City to publicize Trafic. It mentions a special screening
        at The Museum of Modern Art, as well as the fact that Tati
        and his wife were in a minor traffic accident a few days
        after the showing.

231   _____. "Traffic Is Well Worth Getting Into." Daily News
        (12 December).
        A positive review of the film which finds Tati "a bril-
        liant comedic talent."

232   CRIST, JUDITH. "A Honey of a Jam." New York Magazine
        (11 December):74.
        A very positive review of Trafic which ranks Tati with
        Chaplin as "one of the great artists of our time." Crist

sees the film as the "sum of Tati's past work," and remarks
on his decidedly visual wit. She claims that although the
comedy is not hilarious, it is "90 minutes of peaceful,
charming good humor."

233   DALE, R. C. "Two New Tati's." Film Quarterly 26, no. 2
      (Winter):30-32.
         A review of both Trafic and Playtime which finds the
      latter a masterpiece. Dale finds intriguing both Tati's
      themes of the barrenness of contemporary life and his use
      of reflection shots to underscore the relative nature of
      reality. Dale also compares Tati's visual pacing to the
      verbal gags of Hawks, and the organization of Tati's films
      to the work of René Clair. He dismisses Trafic as a "Tatian
      Weekend without politics," and ascribes its "failure" to the
      haste with which the film was made.

234   DAVIES, BRENDA. "Traffic." Monthly Film Bulletin 39, no. 456
      (January):17.
         A plot summary and favorable review of the film. Davies
      considers the camping car to be the real star of the film,
      and notes that Tati treats machines with an anthropomorphic
      eye. She talks of the character of Hulot as being more
      prominent than in Playtime, but "oddly remote." She men-
      tions the participation of Bert Haanstra in the film.

235   DUFOUR, PIE. "Jacques Tati, Noted French Comic Coming for
      Festival." States-Item 96, no. 11 (18 October).
         An article reporting that Tati will be in New Orleans
      the following week (25-31 October) for a festival of his
      films.

236   GAGNARD, FRANK. "Fete Tati." Times Picayune (17 October).
         An article discussing the upcoming Tribute to Tati that
      will begin in New Orleans the following week.

237   GELMIS, JOSEPH. Review of Traffic. Newsday (12 December).
         A short negative review of the film that claims "the
      gags are too few and far between to provide more than a
      few chuckles."

238   GREENSPUN, ROGER. "Traffic." New York Times (12 December):60.
         A very favorable review of Trafic which praises the pre-
      cision of Tati's gag structure and his avoidance of close-
      ups in favor of long-shots.

239   KAEL, PAULINE. Review of Trafic. New Yorker (16 December):
      132.
         A negative short mention of the film which finds Tati's
      gags "fuzzy and only vaguely comic."

1972

240   MONACO, JAMES. "Oldies But Goodies, Materialist Farce:
      Jacques Tati's Traffic and Playtime." Take One 3, no. 11
      (September):40.
          A review of Playtime and Trafic which characterizes the
      films as an important "diptych . . . which summons up the
      twentieth century experience." Monaco finds particular
      parallels between Tati and Godard, seeing Playtime as Tati's
      Two or Three Things . . . and Alphaville, and Trafic as
      Tati's Weekend. He also sees Tati's work as especially
      amenable to structuralist criticism.

241   NESBIT, DOUG. "Trafic." Motion Picture Daily (25 October):3.
          A positive review which finds the film a "delightful
      episodic comedy."

242   PHILLIPS, MCCANDLISH. "Mr. Hulot Stalks Into Town for
      Traffic." New York Times (15 December):56.
          A descriptive piece on Trafic which includes quotes from
      an interview with Tati.

243   SAFRAN, DON. "Tati Debuts Festival." Dallas Times Herald
      (24 October).
          A review of Trafic on the occasion of its opening as
      part of a French film festival in Dallas. Tati attended
      the screening and did an improvisation of policemen in
      France and England. Safran calls Trafic a "brilliant film."

244   SARRIS, ANDREW. "Films in Focus." Village Voice (28 December).
          A positive review of Trafic in which he calls the film
      "Tati's Weekend."

245   THOMAS, KEVIN. "Jacques Tati: Silent Comedy's Heir." Los
      Angeles Times View (24 November).
          An interview with Tati upon the occasion of a retrospec-
      tive of his films at the Filmex Festival in Los Angeles.
      Finding himself in Hollywood, Tati speaks particularly of
      his debt to American silent and sound comedians: Mack
      Sennett, W. C. Fields, the Marx Brothers, Keaton, and
      Chaplin. Thomas claims that Tati received an extraordinar-
      ily enthusiastic response at Filmex.

246   WINSTEN, ARCHER. "Jacques Tati: Film Paces the Madness of
      Traffic." New York Post (12 December).
          A very positive review which calls the film a "Jacques
      Tati world, and wonderful to behold . . . unique . . . and
      . . . as funny as his best one, Mr. Hulot's Holiday."

247   YELLEN, LINDA. "Mr. Hulot (Tati) in Traffic Jam." Hollywood
      Reporter (19 December):8.

A fairly negative review which states that the humor of the film does not "travel well." Although she feels it will be a commercial failure, Yellen thinks it will be a critical success.

1973

248 ANON. "Jacques Tati." In Who's Who in France (Qui est qui en France?) 11th Ed., 1973-1974. Paris: Éditions Jacques Lafitte, p. 1520.
A dictionary/encyclopedia entry on Tati giving fairly detailed biographical data as well as useful information on his stage career, work in films, and awards received.

249 CANBY, VINCENT. "Bravo Chaplin! Bravo Tati!" New York Times (8 July):1, 3.
An article that discusses the exhibition in New York City of Playtime and Monsieur Verdoux, both films that Canby cites as among the "greatest screen comedies of all time." Canby stresses the detail of Playtime and the simultaneity of its gag structure, and remarks how it creates demands on the audience. He also notes its use of sound.

250 _____. "Playtime a Funny Film and Tati's Most Brilliant." New York Times (28 June).
A very positive review of the film which calls it Tati's most brilliant work and a "reckless act of faith." Canby sees it as divided into three set pieces: the airport sequence, the exhibition-hall sequence, and the nightclub act--a "neon-lit gotterdammerung." He also applauds the "density of [its] wit."

251 COCKS, JAY. "Trafic." Time (1 January):37.
A negative review of the film which finds Tati too derivative of the old comic masters, and his performance devoid of "all trace of spontaneity and humanity." Cocks also states that the gags seem "too cherished and worked over" with a "laboratory air about them."

252 DREW, BERNARD. Review of Playtime. Ossining Citizen Register (2 July).
A negative review which finds the film too long and often "wandering."

253 DREXLER, ROSALYN. "Acting Takes All Kinds." Vogue (October).
A positive review of Playtime which finds it ahead of its time. Drexler calls it a masterpiece and says it "should be seen by those who are willing to be entertained in a most original manner."

1973

254   EBERT, ROGER. Review of Trafic. Chicago Sun Times
      (13 February).
          A very positive review of the film which calls it a
      "brilliant new comedy."

255   GALLAGHER, T. A. "Tati's Discombobulated Cosmos." Village
      Voice (2 August):68.
          A positive review of Playtime which sees the film as
      part of the modernist tradition. He quotes Godard as hav-
      ing credited French neo-realism to Tati's Jour de fête, and
      makes the claim that "as Rossellini is to history, Antonioni
      to psychology, Bresson to drama, so is Tati to comedy."

256   GILLIATT, PENELOPE. "Profiles: Playing." New Yorker
      (27 January):35-47.
          An extensive profile/interview with Tati during a festi-
      val of his films in the French Quarter of New Orleans.
      Gilliatt includes interesting anecdotal material from her
      visit with Tati (for example, his dislike of formal func-
      tions and dinner jackets, his desire to eat in the student
      rather than the teacher cafeteria in his visit to a school).
      She also elicits from him a discussion of radical politics,
      his family background, and various aspects of his filmic
      style. Tati talks about the lack of traditional narrative
      in Playtime, the genesis of the Hulot character, his use of
      sound, music, and dialogue, and finally, his interest in
      filmic mise-en-scène. (See also entry 292.)

257   K. C. "Playtime Needles Society." Daily News (28 June).
          A fairly negative review of the film which finds it less
      successful than Les Vacances, Mon oncle, and Trafic.

258   KISSEL, HOWARD. "Playtime." Women's Wear Daily (28 June).
          A negative review of the film which states that it has
      a "listless diffuse quality," and "a total lack of pacing
      or building to comic climaxes."

259   LEACH, D. "Playtime." Films in Review 24 (October):505-6.
          A mixed review of the film which recognizes it as the
      "quintessential Tati effort" but faults it for its "dull
      spots." Leach gives particular attention to Tati's use of
      sound.

260   MAST, GERALD. The Comic Mind. New York: Bobbs-Merrill,
      pp. 293-98.
          Mast speaks of Tati in a chapter on "The Clown Tradition."
      He first discusses Tati in relation to the comic traditions
      of Chaplin and Keaton. He finds Tati's themes and sound
      technique like Chaplin, and his pantomime and shooting style

like Keaton. Mast sees Tati's films as evincing a hostility
to "modernity, inhuman efficiency [and] deadening routine."
He finds the most interesting aspects of Tati's style his
control of the sound track, his long-shot/long-take style,
his brilliant shot composition, and his imaginative sight
gags.

261   MITCHELL, MARTIN. "More Films." After Dark (February).
      A review of Trafic and a discussion of Tati whom Mitchell
      finds the only contemporary comic (aside from Woody Allen)
      who deserves the auteurist label.

262   OUTIE, CLAUDE. "Playtime." France-Amérique (28 June).
      An article discussing the film's exhibition in New York
      City and questioning whether Tati's humor is "exportable."

263   ROSENBAUM, JONATHAN. "Tati's Democracy: An Interview and
      Introduction." Film Comment 9, no. 3 (May-June):36-41.
      An interview with Tati and an introduction to his work.
      Rosenbaum concentrates on Playtime and its status as a revo-
      lutionary cinematic text. He speaks of its radicalization
      of the Bazinian notion of the spectator freedom engendered
      by the long-take format. He notes as well how the film
      overloads the frame and eliminates distinctions between
      "subject and background." Finally, he analyzes the geomet-
      ric construction of Playtime in terms of a conflict between
      regimented straight lines and graceful curves. In the in-
      terview, Tati speaks of Playtime and Trafic. Among the
      topics discussed are his attitude toward contemporary decor
      and technology, his construction of sound tracks, and his
      interest in creating a "democratic" style of comedy.

264   SCHICKEL, RICHARD. "Lifeless Abstractionist." Time
      (6 August).
      A negative review of Playtime which complains of its
      "total lack of narrative drive" and its "air of aimlessness."

265   SCHIER, ERNEST. "Trafic." Philadelphia Evening Bulletin
      (5 April).
      A review of Trafic in which Schier talks of Hulot's
      "built-in hesitation" and of his lack of "synchronization
      compared with the life rhythms of the people around him."

266   TATI, JACQUES. "Govorjat Laureaty Festivalja." Iskusstvo
      Kino, no. 7 (July):26.
      Jacques Tati replies to a questionnaire at the Moscow
      Film Festival. Illustrated.

1973

267   WILLIAMSON, BRUCE.   Review of Trafic.   Playboy (May).
      A lukewarm review of the film.

268   WINSTEN, ARCHER.   "Rages and Outrages."   New York Post
      (8 January).
            Winsten discusses Trafic and interviews Tati on the oc-
      casion of his visit to New York City.   Tati speaks of his
      love for American comedy and claims that Keaton once said,
      "Tati has started where we have stopped."

                              1974

269   CANBY, VINCENT.   "Paris Has Gone Mad Over Movies."   New York
      Times (9 June).
            An article on the French film scene in which Canby men-
      tions Parade, which he finds more a "spectacle" than a film.

*270 CHEVASSU, F.   "Parade."   Revue du Cinéma (Image et Son), no.
      288-289 (October):263.
            Cited in Film/Literature Index/1974 (Albany, N.Y.:
      Filmdex, 1976), p. 369.

271   CH. R.   "Parade: La Joie du cirque."   France-Soir
      (19 December).
            A positive review of the film in which the author men-
      tions how Parade communicates Tati's love for "the unique
      art of the ring" as well as his "tenderness and enthusiasm
      for clown and acrobats."

272   DELAIN, MICHEL.   "Tati à l'encan."   L'Express (29 April):52.
            An article bemoaning the recent auction of the rights
      to Tati's films which were sold for 120,000 francs.   Delain
      cites a debt of 8 million francs incurred on the 15-million
      franc Playtime as the reason for the auction.   Tati is seen
      as a Don Quixote of industrial cinema, and his situation is
      compared to Marcel Carné, who was also denied rights to his
      films.

273   _____.   "Tati a trouvé son parade."   L'Express (23 December):
      8-9.
            An article on Parade and a profile of Tati.   Delain
      speaks of the mime routines Tati performs in the film and
      of his music-hall background.   Tati bemoans the death of
      the circus as a popular art and speaks of his interest in
      opposing the "general notion of the sad clown."

274   KISSEL, HOWARD.   "At Cannes: From Brilliance to Boredom."
      Women's Wear Daily (24 May):32.

1975

In a long article on Cannes, Kissel mentions Parade, which he feels had five minutes of brilliant pantomime, but not enough to redeem the whole film.

275   MOSK.   "Parade."   Variety (22 May).
      A discussion of Parade which the reviewer finds more viable as a television piece than as a film. He mentions its genesis in a Swedish television show and lists the various mime routines Tati performs in the film: the punchy fighter, the prancing horse, the agitated tennis player, and the testy soccer goalie.

*276 PURDY, J.   "Playtime." Movietone News 230, no. 26 (March).
      Cited in Film/Literature Index/1974 (Albany, N.Y.: Filmdex, 1976), p. 381.

277   SIEGEL, JOEL E.   "Playtime." Film Heritage 9, no. 3 (Spring): 35, 36, 40.
      A laudatory review of Playtime which calls it a "visionary work," and "a miracle of a movie." Siegel relates the production circumstances of the work and bemoans its having been cut for American distribution. He examines the film's themes, centering on its critique of contemporary urban design, and lists specific gags involving architecture and international merchandising. Like many critics, Siegel finds admirable the multiplicity of gags occurring simultaneously in Playtime, calling the film a "twenty-ring-circus." He also praises what he terms the three "miracles" which close the film: the traffic jam/carousel, the flower-like traffic lights, and the final shot of the night sky. "The material world," he notes, "has become wholly spiritualized." Siegel ends the piece by noting that when the film audience left the screening of Playtime he attended, they laughed at seeing their reflections in the theater's glass front doors. Thus, he concludes, Tati's comedy has real-world relevance.

1975

278   ANON.   "Jacques Tati." In International Who's Who. 39th Ed., 1975-1976. London: Europa Publications, p. 1718.
      An encyclopedia entry on Tati's life and film career.

279   ANON.   "Parade." Le Nouvel Observateur (January).
      A positive review which calls the film "a little masterpiece of poetic handiwork" and "a universe of sound, form and color."

1975

280   ANON. "Parade." Positif 166 (February):70.
      A short review of the film.

281   CHAUVET, LOUIS. "Parade." Le Figaro (4 January).
      A positive review of the film in which he discusses its
      quality of "nostalgia" and its evocation of music-hall en-
      tertainment.

*282 DUTEIL, C. "Parade." Jeune cinéma 84 (February):32-33.
            Cited in Film/Literature Index 1975 (Albany, N.Y.:
      Filmdex, 1977), p. 411.

*283 GRANT, J. "Parade." Cinéma 195 (February):133.
            Cited in Film/Literature Index/1975 (Albany, N.Y.:
      Filmdex, 1977), p. 411.

284   JOLIVET, NICOLE. "Après Parade Tati prepare Confusion."
      France-Soir (2 January).
            A discussion of Tati's current financial problems and a
      summary of Parade's production circumstances.

285   LACOMBE, ALAIN. "Parade." Écran, no. 33 (February):57-58.
            In a review of Parade, Lacombe describes the film as be-
      ing shot specifically for television format. Thus, Tati
      used several cameras and shot predominantly in long-shot
      with relatively little editing. Lacombe feels that Parade
      is not so much a "Tati film" in the conventional sense, as
      an attempt simply to record and pay homage to the circus.

286   PENNINGTON, RON. "Confusion about Confusion--Tati in
      Hollywood or Europe?" Hollywood Reporter 137, no. 31
      (7 August):1, 21.
            A report that Tati will not make Confusion in Hollywood,
      contrary to what was printed in an earlier article in the
      same journal. (See entry 287.) Tati is quoted as saying
      he is presently trying to make the film as a Franco-Anglo-
      Swedish production.

287   TUSHER, WILL. "Jacques Tati to Make First Hollywood Film."
      Hollywood Reporter 137, no. 21 (24 July).
            A report that Tati will make a film entitled Confusion
      in Hollywood, to be produced by David Frost for Paradine
      Productions.

                              1976

288   ANON. "Tati, le cirque, et le feérie." Le Figaro (9 May).
            A still photograph from Parade, which, it is reported,

is being shown out of competition at the Cannes Film Festival.

289   ARMES, ROY. The Ambiguous Image. Bloomington: Indiana University Press, pp. 69-81.

Armes attempts to situate Tati's work within the context of modernist European narrative cinema. He emphasizes the realism of Tati's comedy, seeing his work as a descendant of the Italian neo-realist school. He sees Tati as an especially important director for having linked the Italian and French schools of cinema. He also discusses other issues in Tati's work: the "democracy" of his comedy and the sparse, discontinuous nature of his narrative line.

290   De BARONCELLI, JEAN. "Un Soir de fête avec Tati." Le Monde (22 December).

An article on Parade and on Tati's recent financial problems. He calls Parade a "modest and poetic" film and mentions its difference from Fellini's melancholy Clowns.

291   FISCHER, LUCY. "Beyond Freedom and Dignity: An Analysis of Jacques Tati's Playtime." Sight and Sound 45 (Autumn): 234-39.

Fischer counters the common claim that because Tati employs a radical long-shot/long-take format, he allows the spectator complete perceptual "freedom." Although she admits that this is true to some degree, she emphasizes the more subterranean ways in which Tati "controls" the viewer within the long-shot/long-take style: through montage within the shot, color, sound, and camera movement. This article operates, as well, as a critique of Bazin's theory of the long-take in the essay, "The Evolution of the Language of Cinema," in What Is Cinema? trans. Hugh Gray (Berkeley: University of California Press, 1967).

292   GILLIATT, PENELOPE. Jacques Tati. London: Woburn Press, 96 pp.

An extended interview with Tati and a reworking of Gilliatt's New Yorker profile of Tati. (See entry 256.) It does however, include more biographical information on his career in the music hall and provides many excellent stills.

293   MONTAIGNE, PIERRE. "Tati s'en va-t-en guerre." Le Figaro (12 May).

An article reporting that Tati is convalescing after several serious operations and is at work on his next film Confusion. Tati is quoted as feeling that in French film production, "creators have less and less opportunity to express themselves."

1976

294　REZOAGLI, SANDRO.　"Il circo di Tati."　Cineforum, no. 153
　　　(March):155-57.
　　　　　A positive review of Parade in which the author acknowl-
　　　edges Tati's extraordinary homage to the spectacle of the
　　　circus, and identifies Tati's fundamental qualities as his
　　　vigorous sense of comic geometry, his tender and joyful
　　　look at reality, and his highly controlled style.

1977

295　A. De G.　"Bonnes vacances de M. Hulot."　Quotidien de Paris
　　　(23 March).
　　　　　A positive review of Les Vacances upon its rerelease.
　　　He comments that Tati proposes "a vacation canvas whose
　　　every point amuses."

296　ALES, B.　"Jacques Tati."　Ciné-revue 57 (April):10.
　　　　　An interview with Tati.

297　ANON.　"Group Repackages Major Tati Films for International
　　　Market."　Variety (23 February).
　　　　　An article telling that Tati's films, formerly in re-
　　　ceivership, were now being repackaged by a group, including
　　　Tati himself.

298　ANON.　Le Figaro (29 May).
　　　　　An article reporting that Tati will appear in Black
　　　Humor, directed by Mauro Bolognini.

299　ANON.　"Mon oncle."　Le Nouvel Observateur (December).
　　　　　A favorable review of Mon oncle, which was having a re-
　　　vival at several Parisian theaters.

300　ANON.　"Mon oncle."　Français (16 December).
　　　　　A plot summary of the film with credits, published dur-
　　　ing its Parisian rerelease.

301　ANON.　"Tati French Film Satirist in London to Promote Reissue
　　　Package of His Pix."　Variety (22 June).
　　　　　An article about the reissue of Les Vacances, Mon oncle,
　　　Jour de fête, and Playtime in London.

*302　CHEVASSU, F.　"Jour de fête."　Revue du Cinéma (Image et Son)
　　　316 (April):94-96.
　　　　　An illustrated review of Jour de fête with credits.
　　　(Cited in Film/Literature Index/1977 (Albany, N.Y.:
　　　Filmdex, 1980), p. 340.

*303 _____. "Les Vacances." Revue du Cinéma (Image et Son) 317
(May):107-9.
An illustrated review of Les Vacances with stills.
Cited in Film/Literature Index/1977 (Albany, N.Y.: Filmdex,
1980), p. 663.

*304 CLEMENT, S., et al. "Dossier: Cinéma et société de
consommation." Cinéma (November):20-35.
An illustrated article on Playtime. Cited in Film/
Literature Index/1977 (Albany, N.Y.: Filmdex, 1980), p. 482.

*305 DECAUX, E. "Les Vacances." Cinématographe 27 (May):32.
An illustrated review of the film with credits. Cited
in Film/Literature Index/1977 (Albany, N.Y.: Filmdex,
1980), p. 663.

306 FABRE, MAURICE. "Après l'échec de Playtime, le triomphe du
festival Tati." France-Soir (14 February).
An article reporting the opening on 16 February of a
Tati festival in Paris with the exhibition of Jour de fête,
Les Vacances, Mon oncle, Playtime, and Trafic. Fabre also
interviews Tati who talks of his previous financial difficulties, his reasons for making films in Sweden and Holland,
and his excitement and fear concerning the rerelease of his
work. He discusses his concern for young cineastes who do
not receive much support and no longer have the vehicle of
short films for their apprenticeship.

307 _____. "Tati en pleine Confusion." France-Soir (14 December).
An article about the current Parisian revival of Jour de
fête and Les Vacances as well as Tati's hopes to make a new
film, Confusion.

308 FLOT, YONNICK. "Le Retour de Jacques Tati." France Amérique
17-23 (February).
An article that discusses the revival of Tati's films
after several years' absence from the screen. It praises
Tati for having always worked "in freedom."

309 FREUND, ANDREAS. "Jacques Tati and His Movies Return after
Enforced Vacation." New York Times (19 February):14.
Freund discusses Tati's "enforced vacation" from the
film world because of his bankruptcy after Playtime. Freund
explains how all Tati's films were impounded by the banks
and reports that finally a French distributor has paid $1.6
million for their release. Tati speaks of his plans for a
new film, Confusion. Freund ends the article by briefly reviewing Tati's career.

Writings about Jacques Tati

1977

*310 LEDERLÉ, J-L. "Jour de fête." Cinématographe 26 (April):32.
An illustrated review of Jour de fête with credits.
Cited in Film/Literature Index/1977 (Albany, N.Y.: Filmdex,
1980), p. 340.

*311 LEFEVRE, R. "Jour de fête." Revue de Cinéma (Image et Son)
no. 320/321 (October):148-49.
Cited in Film/Literature Index/1977 (Albany, N.Y.:
Filmdex, 1980), p. 340.

312 MADDOCK, BRENT. The Films of Jacques Tati. Metuchen, N.J.:
Scarecrow Press, 179 pp.
An extensive, in-depth study of Tati's work. Maddock
attempts not only to discuss Tati's films but to establish
his relation to the history of French and American film
comedy. Thus, he discusses briefly such figures as André
Deed, Max Linder, René Clair, the Prevert Brothers, Chaplin,
Keaton, Lloyd, and Langdon. After briefly summarizing
Tati's early career, he devotes a chapter to each of the
director's five feature films. In succeeding chapters, he
deals with such issues as the themes of Tati's work in general, his overall comic style, and his use of technology.
The book ends with a discussion of Tati's projected work,
Confusion.

*313 SAUVAGET, P. "Les Vacances." Revue du Cinéma (Image et Son)
no. 320/321 (October):291-92.
Cited in Film/Literature Index/1977 (Albany, N.Y.:
Filmdex, 1980), p. 663.

*314 SOREL, S. "Jour de fête." Téléciné, no. 217 (April):40-41.
Cited in Film/Literature Index/1977 (Albany, N.Y.:
Filmdex, 1980), p. 340.

315 THOMPSON, KRISTIN. "Parameters of the Open Film: Les
Vacances de Monsieur Hulot." Wide Angle 2, no. 1:22-30.
Discusses Les Vacances in terms of Noel Burch's notion
of the "open film," a concept he mentions in Theory of Film
Practice (New York: Praeger, 1973). Thompson defines an
"open film" as one that allows its structure to be created
as much by formal as by narrative concerns. He discusses
Les Vacances on stylistic, narrative, and thematic levels
and finds the principle of "overlap" (in editing, sound articulation, and narrative actions) central to the film's
structure.

316 TREMOIS, CLAUDE-MARIE. "Les Vacances . . . Une Si Jolie
Petite Plage." Télérama (13 May):105.
A very positive review of the film which instructs the
viewer to go to the film "to learn to open one's eyes and
ears."

been able to create a bridge between the "popular" and the
"modernist/art" cinema. In addition, Daney discusses Tati's
role as a technical innovator in cinema and, within this
context, states that Parade has not been given its due as
a work of video. Moreover, he claims that Tati's films
have always been about "media" as extensions of the human
body and mind. Finally, in discussing Tati's satirical
comedy, Daney disclaims the notion that Tati attacks modern
technology.

329 HENRY, JEAN-JACQUES. "Claquez vos portes sur un silence d'or."
     Cahiers du Cinéma, no. 303 (September):25-27.
          An article on Tati's use of sound in his films. Henry
     makes the point that Tati has always been a champion of
     technology--color, wide-screen format, video, and sound.
     He also makes the point that in each era in which Tati has
     worked, he has countered the prevalent use of sound. In
     the fifties, when sound tracks were supposed to be "clear,"
     he created a cacophony in Les Vacances. In the sixties,
     when direct, realistic sound was popular, Tati postsynchron-
     ized Playtime with a host of synthetic sounds. Henry also
     talks of Tati's disdain for conventional sound-image rela-
     tionships, and the tendency for Tati's sounds to "fracture"
     the image. Finally, he discusses how stereophonic technol-
     ogy is a necessity for Tati, since it allows him a multi-
     layered, but discrete, mix of sounds.

330 HENRY, JEAN-JACQUES, and LE PÉRON, SERGE. "Entretiens avec
     Tati." Cahiers du Cinéma, no. 303 (September):8-24.
          A two-part interview with Tati. The first part concerns
     his use of sound. Tati speaks of Chaplin's mistake in using
     sound only to talk, rather than exploiting its full possi-
     bilities. He describes his own method which involves avoid-
     ing direct sound and, instead, "casting" sounds when the
     film is done. He also speaks of his interest in stereo-
     phonic sound and decries the fact that more theaters are
     not equipped for it. The second interview treats a variety
     of subjects: the spectator's response to Playtime, the evo-
     lution from geometric to circular blocking patterns in the
     film, and the reason for the film's lack of success in
     France (which Tati credits to the minimization of Hulot).
     Tati also speaks of his use of nonprofessional actors and
     of his method of directing performers in different "planes"
     of the shot. Also discussed are the problems of exhibiting
     films in America, world politics, and the problems of con-
     temporary young filmmakers.

331 HEYMANN, DANIÈLE, and DELAIN, MICHEL. "Tati: Méfiez vous
     des comique anoblis!" L'Express (2 June):21-23.

1979

An interview in which Tati speaks of such issues as his
use of 70mm in Playtime, his financial problems following
that film, and his comedy of observation. He also discusses
his trip to Hollywood in 1959 to receive his Oscar for Mon
oncle, and his meeting with Mack Sennett, Buster Keaton,
Harold Lloyd, and Stan Laurel.

332   SCHEFER, JEAN-LOUIS. "La Vitrine." Cahiers du Cinéma, no.
      303 (September):30.
      An article on the general world view proposed in Tati's
films which Schefer likens alternately to a display case,
an aquarium, and a crystal ball with figures encased within. Thus Schefer stresses the static, arrested, mechanical
sense of life portrayed in Tati's films, as opposed to the
dynamic sense of conventional narration. He also sees characters in Tati's films as merely "bearers of stereotypes,"
going through cliché motions. Summing up, Schefer writes:
"Unless the world destroys itself, like the restaurant in
Playtime, each bearer of gesture remains encased in his
zone of performance, like Flemish gnomes in their crystal
ball. This world hides nothing behind it: it is a glass
display case."

333   THOMPSON, KRISTIN. "Playtime: Comedy on the Edge of
      Perception." Wide Angle 3, no. 2:18-25.
      Thompson argues that Playtime challenges the style of
classical Hollywood cinema (in which the comedies of Chaplin,
Keaton, Lloyd were realized) and fashions an alternative,
modernist mode of organization. Thompson argues that this
style encourages a form of "uncertainty" on the part of the
spectator, since Playtime is "perpetually ungraspable," and
"emphasizes its own excess to an unusual degree." It also
"invites our perceptual engagement with the film at every
level." Thompson then goes on to discuss the perceptual
complexity of the film and its nontraditional gag structure. She argues that Playtime shifts the focus of the
spectator's attention beyond the film into the world of
everyday existence, and therefore has broader social
implications.

1980

334   FIESCHI, JEAN-ANDRÉ. "Jacques Tati." Translated by Michael
      Graham. In Cinema: A Critical Dictionary. Edited by
      Richard Roud. Vol. 2. New York: Viking Press, pp. 1000-1005.
      A critical summary of Tati's career which places him
within the tradition of cinematic "constructors" whose pri-
mary interest is in "structural play." Furthermore, Fieschi
finds Tati's mode of film organization almost "musical" involving "variable and fixed terms, themes, and variations."

Fieschi also discusses Hulot's status as a descendant of
"moon-struck white clowns," like Laurel, Keaton, and
Langdon, and notes the sense of "nostalgia" in Tati's work.
He emphasizes the realism of Tati's comedy, but, nonetheless, points out the high degree of "strangeness" involved
in his work. Fieschi also mentions Tati's innovative use
of sound and his radicalization of the traditional gag
structure.

335 FISCHER, LUCY. "Playtime: The Comic Film as Game." West
Virginia University Philological Papers 26 (August):83-88.
Fischer discusses the comic structure of Playtime and
likens the organization of the film to a cinematic "puzzle"
or "game." She relates this formal issue to the themes of
leisure and play in Tati's work, and to the comic theory of
Henri Bergson. Fischer also likens certain visual strategies in Playtime to children's "pen and pencil" games.

336 INNES, BRIAN. "Jour de fête." The Movie: The Illustrated
History of the Cinema, (Chapter 26):518-19.
A brief discussion of Jour de fete with credits and
frame enlargements. Innes finds the film an early "masterpiece" and claims that it shows the influence of Jean
Renoir. Innes discusses Tati's career in general, and
notes the technological innovations of Jour de fête: its
use of tape-recorded sound, location shooting, and "Thomson-
Color."

337 NURIDSANY, MICHEL. "Vacances avec M. Hulot." Le Figaro
(21 August).
An article about a current Tati festival at Le Grande
Pavois cinema in Paris. Nuridsany feels that, although
Tati has made only four major feature films, each is "perfect." He speaks as well of Tati's use of montage which he
compares to that of Welles, and his use of sound which he
compares to that of Polanski and Godard. He ends by call-
ing Tati a "classic."

338 STRICK, PHILIP. "The Gentle Anarchy of Jacques Tati." In
The Movie: The Illustrated History of the Cinema, (Chapter
40):794-95.
A general survey of Tati's work from his early short
films through Trafic. Strick calls the character of Hulot
a "gentle anarchist" who "was the model for a decade of
drop-outs." He compares Tati's interest in the anti-hero
to that of the early Godard, and his use of architecture
to that of Antonioni.

339 TATI, JACQUES. "The Cinema According to Tati." In Mimes on

1980

>Miming. Edited by Bari Rolfe. Los Angeles and San
>Francisco: Panjandrum Books, pp. 154-57.
>Tati discusses his comic style and his mode of creating
>characters and scenarios. The text is excerpted from pre-
>viously published articles on Tati and is not newly solic-
>ited material.

1981

340 BAZIN, ANDRÉ. "Mr. Hulot and Time." Translated by Walter
Albert.
See this volume, Chapter VIII. For original citations
of the essay in French, see entries 31 and 203.

341 WHITE, MIRIAM. "The Texture of Sound and Surfaces of Humor
in Jacques Tati's Playtime." Paper presented at the Annual
Conference of the Society for Cinema Studies, 21-24 April,
New York City. Abstracted in 1981 Annual Conference,
Society for Cinema Studies, April 21-24, p. 24. New York:
College of Staten Island/CUNY.
According to White's own published abstract, the "paper
focuses on the uses and functions of sound in . . .
Playtime. Two main issues are emphasized in the analysis:
1) the film proposes alternatives to and inversion of conventional "realistic" sound practices; 2) sound becomes an
analyzer of the image. Through these practices Playtime's
status as a referential system becomes blocked. Sound and
image clarify and designate one another rather than working
together to refer to, or constitute an 'external reality.'
The analysis also considers the narrative context of the
film's sound practices, in which causal connections are
displaced by a fortuitous, aleatory pattern of development.
Viewer expectations are not simply thwarted, nor simply re-
organized by an 'alternative' system. Rather, there is a
continual reordering of experience, and deferral of system
and an emphasis on surfaces, textures, and repetition. The
work of Giles Deleuze on nomadism is brought in as a theoretical orientation which helps illuminate the implications
of the film's textual operations."

V. Performances, Writings, and Other Film-Related Activity

Note: Where writings by and interviews with Tati have been annotated previously in Chapter IV, they have been cross-referenced to the earlier entry.

342   Oscar, champion de tennis (1931-32), as Oscar, the tennis
          champion. Dir.: Jacques Tati.

343   On demande une brute (1934), as a timid henpecked husband who
          fights a wrestling match under the guise of being a champ-
          ion. Dir.: Jacques Tati.

344   Gai dimanche (1935), as a "luckless dandy" who goes on a picnic
          with a salesman friend. Dir.: Jacques Tati.

345   Soigne ton gauche (1936), as a farmhand who watches a boxer in
          training and imitates him. Dir.: Jacques Tati.

346   Retour à la terre (1936), role unspecified. Dir.: Jacques
          Tati.

347   Sylvie et le fantôme (1945), as the ghost of a handsome hunter,
          killed some hundred years earlier. Dir.: Claude Autant-
          Lara.

348   Le Diable au corps (1946), as a soldier celebrating the signing
          of the Armistice in a bar. Dir.: Claude Autant-Lara.

349   L'École des facteurs (1947), as François, a village postman.
          Dir.: Jacques Tati.

350   Jour de fête (1949), as François, a village postman. Dir.:
          Jacques Tati.

351   Les Vacances de Monsieur Hulot (1953), as M. Hulot, a vacationer at a seaside resort. Dir.: Jacques Tati.

352   Mon oncle (1958), as M. Hulot, the unemployed brother of
Madame Arpel and uncle to Gérard. Dir.: Jacques Tati.

353   Playtime (1967), as M. Hulot, a Parisian resident who pursues
a business appointment with M. Giffard. Dir.: Jacques
Tati.

354   Trafic (1971), as M. Hulot, an automobile designer for the
Altra Company. Dir.: Jacques Tati.

355   Parade (1973), as M. Loyal, the ringmaster of a circus. Dir.:
Jacques Tati.

STAGE PERFORMANCES

356   From 1931 to 1939, Tati performed his sports mime act in various music halls and clubs in France and other European
countries. Some of the specific appearances mentioned in
Tati biographies are Racing Club Revue (1931), Gerny's
(1933), L'A.B.C. (1936), Casino de Brides-les-Bains (1936),
London Casino (1936), and Mayfair Hotel (1937).

TELEVISION PERFORMANCES

357   "Fanfare," National Broadcasting Company, U.S.A. (1954).
Produced and directed by Max Liebman.

358   Parade shown on Swedish television (1973).

359   Parade shown on French television (1973).

WRITINGS

360   Tati, Jacques. "Les Réveillons de M. Hulot." L'Aurore
(19 December 1953).

361   Tati, Jacques. "Pas d'histoires." Arts, no. 402 (13 March
1953):1, 4.

362   Tati, Jacques. "Un Scène de Vacances de Monsieur Hulot."
La Parisienne (June 1953):833-37.

363   Tati, Jacques. "Il y a erreur sur la personne." Cahiers du
cinéma, no. 42 (December 1954):49. (See entry 61.)

364   Tati, Jacques. "Spectacle permanent." Positif, no. 9
       (December 1954):2-6.

365   Tati, Jacques. "Mon oncle . . . et moi." Unifrance Film
       (March 1958).

366   Tati, Jacques. "Jacques Tati raconte son nouveau film Mon
       oncle." Arts, no. 663 (26 March 1958):6. (See entry 126.)

367   Tati, Jacques. "Govorjat Foaureaty Festvalja." Iskusstvo
       Kino, no. 7 (July 1973):26. (See entry 266.)

368   Tati, Jacques. "Confusion." Proposal for film, 1975. Un-
       published.

369   Tati, Jacques. "The Cinema According to Tati." In Mimes on
       Miming. Edited by Bari Rolfe. Los Angeles and San
       Francisco: Panjandrum Books, 1980. (See entry 339.)

INTERVIEWS

370   Mazarin, C. "Les gags font oublier le scènario." Ciné-Club
       (March 1950).

371   Castex, P. [Interview with Tati.] Les Lettres Françaises,
       no. 394 (12 February 1953).

372   ANON. "Questions sur les Vacances." Elle (May 1953).

373   ANON. [Interview with Tati.] Télérama (Radio-Cinéma)
       (15 August 1954).

374   ANON. [Interview with Tati.] France-USA (December 1954).

375   Morandini, Morando. "Il mimo Tati legge gli uomini." Cinema
       (Rome), no. 135 (10 June 1954):333. (See entry 57.)

376   Buchwald, Art. "Jacques 'Hulot' Tati's American Spectacular."
       New York Herald Tribune (23 August 1955):4. (See entry 65.)

377   Chardère, B. "Jacques Tati." Cinéma 55, no. 3 (January 1955):
       45-47. (See entry 66.)

378   ANON. [Interview with Tati.] L'Humanité (28 March 1956).

379   Guth, P. "J'ai vu Tati tourner son prochain film." Le Figaro
       Littéraire (29 September 1956):4. (See entry 71.)

380   Kryou, Ado. [Interview with Tati.] Cinéma 56 (October-
       November 1956):9.

381 Truffaut, François. "Tati: Connaissez-vous Mon oncle." Arts, no. 580 (8 August 1956):1, 3. (See entry 74.)

382 Anon. "Make Them Laugh." Films and Filming 3, no. 11 (August 1957):15. (See entry 75.)

383 Anon. [Interview with Tati.] Image et Son (December 1957):15.

384 Monod, Martine. "Jacques Tati ou le passioné raissonable." Les Lettres Françaises, no. 693 (24 October 1957):1, 5. (See entry 80.)

385 Anon. [Interview with Tati.] Los Angeles Times (15 December 1958).

386 Anon. [Interview with Tati.] Paris-Presse (20 May 1958).

387 Anon. "Mon oncle." Cinéma 58 (June 1958):28. (See entry 88.)

388 Bazin, André, and Truffaut, François. "Entretien avec Jacques Tati." Cahiers du cinéma, no. 83 (May 1958):2-20. (See entry 95.)

389 Buchwald, Art. "Art Buchwald in Paris: Brigitte and Tati." New York Herald Tribune. (16 October 1958). (See entry 98.)

390 Dubreuilh, S. [Interview with Tati.] Les Lettres Françaises (2 May 1958).

391 Ganne, Gilbert. "Tati sans camera." Les Nouvelles Littéraires, no. 1605 (5 June 1958):8. (See entry 108.)

392 Martini, Stelio. "Sospetto per il Signor Hulot." Cinema Nuovo (Milan), no. 135 (September-October 1958):107. (See entry 115.)

393 Nason, Richard W. "M. Tati in Praise of Innocence and Smiles." New York Times (2 November 1958). (See entry 119.)

394 Ross, Don. "Tati's Mr. Hulot on Screen Again." New York Herald Tribune (2 November 1958). (See entry 121.)

395 Slocum, Bill. "Americans Are Nuts But Nice, Tati Says." New York Mirror (28 October 1958). (See entry 125.)

396 Thirer, Irene. "Movie Spotlight." New York Post (3 November 1958). (See entry 127.)

397 Anon. "French Comic Says U.S. Forgets How to Laugh." New York Herald Tribune (26 April 1959). (See entry 132.)

398   Anon. "Jacques Tati Overwhelmed on Visit to Film Capital."
       Newark Evening News (15 April 1959). (See entry 134.)

399   Suffert, G. [Interview with Tati.] Témoinage Chrétien
       (8 May 1959).

400   Baby, Y. [Interview with Tati.] Le Monde (17 February 1962).

401   Anon. "Voyage à Tativille." Cinéma, no. 99 (September-
       October 1965):16-22. (See entry 157.)

402   Anon. "Journey to Tativille." Sight and Sound (Autumn 1965):
       162. (See entry 156.)

403   Lennon, Peter. "M. Hulot Recruits Army Wives." New York Times
       (13 March 1966). (See entry 160.)

404   Natta, Enzo. "Tativille: Incontro con Jacques Tati."
       Cineforum, no. 54 (April 1966):299-303. (See entry 161.)

405   Chalon, Jean. "Avec Playtime, son 'come-back' Tati a-t-il
       realisé son 'hit et demi'?" Le Figaro Littéraire
       (11 December 1967). (See entry 168.)

406   Lenoir, Thomas. "Tati et le temps des loisirs," L'Express
       (30 January-5 February 1967):30-32. (See entry 177.)

407   Mourlet, M. [Interview with Tati.] Les Nouvelles Littéraires,
       no. 2100 (30 November 1967):16.

408   Mourlet, M. "Les confidences de M. Hulot." Les Nouvelles
       Littéraires, no. 2104 (28 December 1967):14. (See entry
       181.)

409   Trémois, C. M. [Interview with Tati.] Télérama (Radio-Cinéma)
       (17 December 1967).

410   Anon. "Playtime: Le Nouveau Film de Jacques Tati." Cinema
       international, no. 77 (1968):761. (See entry 186.)

411   Anon. "Tati." Cahiers du Cinéma, no. 199 (March 1968):8-20.
       (See entry 188.)

412   Anon. "Vers un livre blanc du cinéma français." Cahiers du
       Cinéma, no. 200-201 (April-May 1968):92-93.

413   Hart, Denis. "How Jacques Tati Made the English Laugh."
       Daily Telegraph (2 August 1968). (See entry 195.)

414   Woodside, Harold. "Tati Speaks." Take One 2, no. 6 (July-
       August 1969):6-8. (See entry 204.)

415   Anon. [Interview with Tati.] <u>Manchester Guardian</u> (19 November 1971).

416   Anon. [Interview with Tati.] <u>Cinéma 9</u>, no. 17 (October-November 1971):11-14.

417   Anon. [Interview with Tati.] <u>Jeune cinéma</u>, no. 56 (June-July 1971):15-18.

418   Carroll, Kathleen. "M. Hulot Is a Loser in the Modern World." <u>Sunday News</u> (26 November 1972):28. (See entry 230.)

419   Drouzy, M., and Hansen, P. E. "Samtale and Jacques Tati." <u>Kusmora</u> 18, no. 107 (February 1972):92-95.

420   Phillips, McCandlish. "Mr. Hulot Stalks into Town for <u>Traffic</u>." <u>New York Times</u> (15 December 1972):56. (See entry 242.)

421   Thomas, Kevin. "Jacques Tati: Silent Comedy's Heir." <u>Los Angeles Times View</u> (24 November 1972). (See entry 245.)

422   Gilliatt, Penelope. "Profiles: Playing." <u>New Yorker</u> (27 January 1973):35-47. (See entry 256.)

423   Rosenbaum, Jonathan. "Tati's Democracy." <u>Film Comment</u> 9, no. 3 (May-June 1973):36-41. (See entry 263.)

424   Winsten, Archer. "Rages and Outrages." <u>New York Post</u> (8 January 1973). (See entry 268.)

425   Delain, Michel. "Tati a trouvé son parade." <u>L'Express</u> (23 December 1974):8-9. (See entry 273.)

426   Gilliatt, Penelope. <u>Jacques Tati</u>. London: Woburn Press, 1976. (See entry 292.)

427   Fabre, Maurice. "Après l'échec de <u>Playtime</u>, le triomphe du festival Tati." <u>France-Soir</u> (14 February 1977). (See entry 306.)

428   Montaigne, Pierre. "Les imprécations de M. Hulot." <u>Le Figaro</u> (29-30 July 1978). (See entry 321.)

429   Henry, Jean-Jacques, and LePéron, Serge. "Entretiens avec Jacques Tati." <u>Cahiers du Cinéma</u>, no. 303 (September 1979): 8-24. (See entry 330.)

430   Heymann, Danièle, and Delain, Michel. "Tati: Méfiez vous des comiques 'anoblis.'" <u>L'Express</u> (2 June 1979):21-23. (See entry 331.)

VI. Archival Sources

In pursuing archival research on the films of Jacques Tati, I wrote to all members of the Fédération Internationale des Archives du Film and to several FIAF "observers." Below are listed those archives that responded with either film or print material (books, clippings, journal articles) on Tati. Certain archives had no materials; others did not respond to my survey. Use of all materials is subject to the particular institutions' regulations and restrictions.

AUSTRALIA

431   National Film Archive, National Library of Australia, Parkes Place, Canberra 2600.
      Print materials
      Stills

CANADA

432   La Cinémathèque Québécoise, 335 Boul De Maissonneuve Est, Montréal, Québec H2X 1K1.
      Films: <u>Sylvie et le fantôme</u>
      Print materials

433   National Film, Television and Sound Archives, 395 Wellington Street, Ottawa K1A ON3.
      Print materials
      Stills

DENMARK

434   Det Danske Filmuseum, St. Søndervoldstraede, 1419 Copenhagen K.
      Print material

Archival Sources

435   National Film Archive, 81 Dean Street, London W1V 6AA.
        Films: Jour de fête, Sylvie et le Fantôme, Le Diable
    au corps
        Print material
        Stills

FINLAND

436   Finnish Film Archive, (Suomen Elokuva-Arkisto), Luotsikatu 13,
    00160 Helsinki 16.
        Films: Mon oncle
        Print material

FRANCE

437   Centre National de la Cinématographie, Service Des Archives
    Du Film, 78390 Bois D'Arcy.
        Films: On demande une brute (negative), Soigne ton
    gauche (negative), Retour à la terre (negative), L'École
    des facteurs (positive), Jour de fête (negative), Trafic
    (negative), Parade (positive), Sylvie et le fantôme (posi-
    tive and negative), Le Diable au corps (positive and nega-
    tive).

438   Cinémathèque de Toulouse, 3 rue Roquelaine, Toulouse 31000.
        Films: Gai dimanche, Soigne ton gauche, L'École des
    facteurs, Jour de fête, Les Vacances de Monsieur Hulot,
    Sylvie et le fantôme, Le Diable au corps
        Print material
        Stills

439   Cinémathèque Universitaire, U.E.R. d'Art de D'Archéologie,
    3 rue Michelet, 75006 Paris.
        Films: Jour de fête, Les Vacances de Monsieur Hulot,
    Trafic
        Print material

GERMANY (EAST)--(DEUTSCHE DEMOKRATISCHE REPUBLIK)

440   Stiftung Deutsche Kinemathek, Pommernallee 1, 1 Berlin 19.
        Films: Jour de fête, Les Vacances de Monsieur Hulot,
    Mon oncle, Le Diable au corps
        Print material

Archival Sources

GERMANY (WEST)--(BUNDESREPUBLIK DEUTSCHLAND)

441   Deutsches Institut Fur Filmkunde, Schloss, 6200 Wiesbaden-
      Biebrich.
            Print material

INDIA

442   National Film Archive of India, Law College Road, Poona
      411004.
            Films: Les Vacances de Monsieur Hulot
            Print material

ISRAEL

443   Israel Film Archive (Archion Yisraeli Leseratim), 43
      Jabotinsky str., Jerusalem.
            Films: Les Vacances de Monsieur Hulot, Le Diable au
      corps
            Print material

ITALY

444   Cineteca Italiana, Villa Communale, Via Palestro 16, 20121
      Milano.
            Print material

445   Cineteca Nazionale, Centro Sperimentale Di Cinematografia,
      Via Tuscolana 1524, 00173 Roma.
            Films: Jour de fête, Mon oncle, Playtime (dubbed in
      Italian)

446   Museo Nazionale Del Cinema, Piazza San Giovanni 2, 10122
      Torino.
            Print material
            Posters

MEXICO

447   Cineteca Nacional De Mexico, Calzeda de Tlalpan, 1670 Mexico
      21, D.F.
            Films: Mon oncle
            Print material

Archival Sources

448   Nederlands Filmmuseum, Vondelpark 3, 1071 AA Amsterdam.
          Print material

NORWAY

449   Norsk Filminstitutt, Aslakveien 14b, Postbox 5, Oslo 7.
          Print material

POLAND

450   Filmoteka Polska, Ul. Pulawska 61, 00975 Warszawa.
          Print material
          Stills
          Posters

PORTUGAL

451   Cinemateca Portuguesa, Instituto Portugues De Cinema, Rue de
          S. Pedro de Alcantara 45, 1200 Lisboa.
          Print material

SWITZERLAND

452   Cinémathèque Suisse, 12 Place de la Cathédrale, Case Ville
          2512, 1000 Lausanne.
              Films: Jour de fête, Playtime, Le Diable au corps, Trafic
          Print material

UNITED STATES

453   American Film Institute, Charles K. Feldman Library, 501
          Doheny Road, Beverly Hills, Calif. 90210.
          Print material

454   Library of Congress, Motion Picture, Broadcast and Recorded
          Sound Division, Washington, D.C. 20540.
              Films: Le Diable au corps (incomplete negative)
          Print material

455   The Museum of Modern Art, Department of Film, 11 West 53
          Street, New York, N.Y. 10019.
              Films: Sylvie et le fantôme
          Print material
          Stills

144

456   Pacific Film Archives, University Art Museum, University of
           California, Berkeley, Berkeley, Calif.
               Print material

457   UCLA Film Archives, Department of Theater Arts, University of
           California, Los Angeles, Los Angeles, Calif.   90024.
               Films: Les Vacances de Monsieur Hulot
               Print material (Theater Arts Library)

U.S.S.R.

458   Gosfilmofond, Stancia Bielye Stolby, Moskovskaia Oblast.
               Print material
               Stills

VII. Film Distributors

459   Budget Films, 4590 Santa Monica Blvd., Los Angeles, Calif.
      90020. 213/660-0187
          Mr. Hulot's Holiday (Les Vacances de Monsieur Hulot),
          Playtime

460   Em Gee Films, 6924 Canby Avenue, Suite 103, Reseda, Calif.
      91335. 213/981-5506
          Mr. Hulot's Holiday (Les Vacances de Monsieur Hulot)

461   Films Incorporated, 440 Park Avenue South, New York, N.Y.
      10016. 212/889-7910
          Sylvie and the Phantom (Sylvie et le fantôme)

462   Images Film Archive, 300 Phillips Park Road, Mamaroneck, N.Y.
      10543. 800/431-1774; 914/381-2993
          Jour de fête
          Mr. Hulot's Holiday (Les Vacances de Monsieur Hulot)
          Playtime

463   Kit Parker Films, P.O. Box 227, Carmel Valley, Calif. 93924.
      800/538-5838; 408/659-3474 or 659-4131
          Mr. Hulot's Holiday (Les Vacances de Monsieur Hulot)

464   Select Films, 115 West 31st Street, New York, N.Y. 10001.
      212/594-4457
          Mr. Hulot's Holiday (Les Vacances de Monsieur Hulot)
          Playtime

465   Swank Motion Pictures, 60 Bethpage Road, Hicksville, N.Y.
      11801. 516/931-7500
          Traffic (Trafic)

466   Twyman Films, 4700 Wadsworth Road, Box 605, Dayton, Ohio
      45401. 800/543-9594; 513/276-5941
          Mr. Hulot's Holiday (Les Vacances de Monsieur Hulot)
          Playtime
          Traffic (Trafic)

VIII. Appendix
"Mr. Hulot and Time" by André Bazin, translated by Walter Albert

It is a commonplace to state how little genius French film has--
or has had, at least, in the last thirty years--for comedy. Remember
that it was in France, in the first years of the century, that slapstick was born, and it found its exemplary hero in Max Linder, whose
formula was continued by Mack Sennett in Hollywood. There it flour-
ished in the molding of such actors as Harold Lloyd, Harry Langdon,
Buster Keaton, Laurel and Hardy, and above all, Charlie Chaplin. We
know that Chaplin acknowledged Max Linder as his master; yet French
slapstick (if one excepts Max Linder's last films made in Hollywood)
failed, for all practical purposes, to survive the 1914 period and
was subsequently snowed under by the devastating, justified success
of American comedy. Even apart from Chaplin, Hollywood has remained
since the talkies the master of film comedy--first in the slapstick
tradition, regenerated and enriched by W. C. Fields, the Marx Brothers,
and even, on the second level, Laurel and Hardy, while a new theater-
like genre appeared: "American comedy."

In France, on the other hand, sound served only to tempt a disas-
trous adaptation of Boulevard vaudeville. If you wonder what has
happened in comedy since the thirties, you can scarcely find more
than two actors, Raimu and Fernandel; but--more curious still--these
two holy monsters of laughter played only in bad films. Were it not
for Pagnol and his legacy of four or five worthwhile films, one could
not cite a single reel worthy of their gifts, with the possible excep-
tion of the curious, unappreciated François 1er of Christian Jaque
with the addition, for good measure, of the attractive but slight

----

This article originally appeared in French as "Pas de scenario
pour M. Hulot" in Esprit (July 1953):90-95 (See entry 31). It was
reprinted in Qu'est ce que le cinéma?, vol. 1 (Paris: Éditions du
Cerf, 1969, pp. 109-15 under the title "M. Hulot et le temps." Per-
mission was granted to translate the essay into English by the
University of California Press.

creation of Noël-Noël. It is significant that after the failure of
Le Dernier Milliardaire in 1934, René Clair left the French studios
for England and then Hollywood. You can see, then, that what was
lacking in French film was not only gifted actors but a style, a comic idea.

I have purposely avoided mentioning the only original attempt to
revive the French slapstick tradition, that of the Prévert brothers.
Some claim to see in L'Affaire est dans le sac, Adieu Léonard, and
Le Voyage Surprise a renaissance of the comic film. They see these
as misunderstood works of genius. I cannot--any more than the public
which rejected them--bring myself to believe this. Certainly their
work was an interesting try, a sympathetic one, but doomed to failure
because of its intellectualism. With the Préverts, the gag is always
an idea whose visualization comes after the fact, the humor a delayed
reaction which follows the mental process working from the visual gag
to its intellectual intention. It is the method of stories without
words, and it is also why one of our best comic draftsmen, Maurice
Henry, never succeeded in making any headway in films as a gagman.
To this overly intellectual structure, which only arouses laughter on
the rebound, you must add the somewhat grating nature of a humor which
demands of the spectator an undeserved complicity. Film comedy--like,
undoubtedly, theatrical comedy--cannot work without a certain shared
generosity; the private joke is not its domain. Only one film derived
from this Prevertian humor outstrips their intermittent inspiration
and approaches success: that is Drôle de drame. Even here, however,
other frames of reference enter into it, and Marcel Carné usefully
remembered The Beggar's Opera and was inspired by English humor.

Against this wretched historical background, Jour de fête was a
success as unexpected as it was exceptional. Everyone knows the story
of this film, which was made almost illicitly and most economically
and which no distributor wanted to touch. It was the best-seller of
the year and grossed ten times its cost.

Tati became famous at once. But one might wonder if the success
of Jour de fête did not, in fact, exhaust its author's genius. There
were some sensational bits in it--an original comic vein--although,
in fact, it rediscovered the best inspiration of slapstick cinema.
On the one hand, it was said that if Tati had had real genius, he
ought not to have vegetated for twenty years in music halls; on the
other hand, the very originality of the film raised the fear that its
author might not be able to sustain it a second time. One could imagine a series of further adventures of the popular postman (like the
return of Don Camillo) which would serve only to make one regret that
Tati did not have the wisdom to stop where he did.

Now not only did Tati not exploit the character that he had created and whose popularity was a gold mine, but he took four years to
give us his second film which, far from suffering by comparison, rele-
gates Jour de fête to the position of rough draft. The importance

of <u>Les Vacances de Monsieur Hulot</u> should not be underestimated. It
is not only the most important comic work in world film since the
Marx Brothers and W. C. Fields, it is an event in the history of sound
film.

Like all the great comics, Tati--before he makes us laugh--creates
a universe. A world is created from his character, crystallizing like
the supersaturated solution around the grain of salt that is thrown
into it. He can be absent personally from the most comic gags because
M. Hulot is only the metaphysical incarnation of a disorder which en-
dures long after he has passed by.

However, if you step away from the character, you can see at once
that his originality, in comparison with the Commedia dell'arte tradition which continues throughout slapstick, consists of a kind of in-
completion. The Commedia dell'arte hero represents a comic essence
whose function is clear and always like itself. The essence of M.
Hulot, on the contrary, seems to be to dare not to exist at all. He
is a walking distraction, a circumspectness of being. He raises tim-
idity to the level of an ontological principle! But naturally that
very lightness of M. Hulot's touch on the world will be the cause of
all the catastrophes because it is never applied according to the
rules of propriety and social efficacy. M. Hulot has the genius of
gratuitousness, but that is not to say that he is gauche and awkward.
On the contrary, M. Hulot is all grace; he is the Angel Hurluberlu,
and the disorder that he introduces is that of tenderness and freedom.
It is significant that the only characters in the film who are at once
graceful and totally sympathetic are children. This is because they
alone are not doing "vacation homework." To them M. Hulot is not as-
tonishing; he is their brother, always available and, like them, un-
aware of the false shame of the game and the foreshadowings of pleasure. If there is only one dancer at the masked ball, it will be M.
Hulot, peacefully indifferent to the emptiness which surrounds him.
If someone has, on the orders of the retired Commandant, arranged for
a supply of fireworks, M. Hulot's match will ignite the explosive.

But what would M. Hulot be without his holiday? For all the other
temporary inhabitants of this odd resort, one can ideally imagine a
profession, or at least a job. One could assign a place of origin to
those cars and trains which converge (at the beginning of the film)
on that X-by-the-Sea and populate it as if at some mysterious signal.
But M. Hulot's Amilcar has no specific age and, to tell the truth,
comes from nowhere; it is outside of time. One could willingly imagine M. Hulot himself disappearing for ten months out of the year, only
to reappear spontaneously, fading in on 1 July when the time clocks
finally stop. In certain privileged places along the shore and in
the mountains, a provisional time takes shape, in parentheses, a fee-
bly whirling duration turning back on itself, like the cycle of the
tides. It is time consisting of the repetition of useless gestures,
scarcely moving, stagnating at siesta time, but also a ritual Time,
set by the vain liturgy of a conventional pleasure more rigorous than

office time.

That is why there could be no scenario for M. Hulot. A story implies a meaning, a temporal orientation proceeding from cause to effect, with a beginning and an end. On the contrary, Les Vacances de
Monsieur Hulot can only be a succession of events coherent in their
meaning and dramatically independent. Each of the hero's adventures
and misadventures begins, in effect, with the formula: "Another time
M. Hulot . . ." Never before had Time so extensively been the material, almost the object itself, of film. Even more so than in those
experimental films which last the time of the action, M. Hulot clari-
fies for us the temporal dimension of our movements.

In this universe on vacation, timed acts take on an absurd character. Only M. Hulot is never on time because only he lives the
fluidity of this time where others try desperately to re-establish
an empty order: the order to which the click of the restaurant's
swinging door gives a rhythm. They succeed only in thickening time
to the consistency of that still warm, slowly stretching taffy which
so torments M. Hulot, himself a Sisyphus of that caramel paste whose
fall in the dust perpetually renews his imminence.

But the sound track, even more than this image, gives the film
its temporal density. It is also Tati's greatest and technically
most original inspiration. Although some have thought that the sound
track was put together as a kind of sonorous magma on which sentence
fragments pop up intermittently, words all the more ridiculous for
their precision, that is only an erroneous impression made on an in-
attentive ear. As a matter of fact, although there the gag is realistic, indistinct sound elements—like the directions from the station
amplifier—are rare. On the contrary, the essence of Tati's astute-
ness is the destruction of clarity by clarity. The dialogue is in no
way incomprehensible; it is, rather, insignificant and this insignifi-
cance is revealed by its very precision. Tati manages this principal-
ly by distorting loudness relationships between sound levels, sometimes going so far as to impose the sound from an off-camera scene
on a mute sequence. In general, his sound track is made up of realistic elements: fragments of dialogue, cries, and various reflective
comments—none of them set rigorously in a dramatic situation. In
relation to this background, an ill-timed noise takes on a deceptive
importance. Take, for example, that evening at the hotel where the
boarders are reading, discussing or playing cards: Hulot is playing
Ping-Pong and his celluloid ball makes a jarring noise, shattering
the relative silence like a pool ball; with every bounce, we seem to
hear it growing larger. At the base of this film, against an authentic sound track actually recorded on a beach, are imposed artificial
sounds that are no less precise but are constantly out of synchroni-
zation. From the combination of this realism and these distortions
is born the irrefutable sound inanity of this still human world.
There is no doubt that the physical aspect of speech, its "anatomy,"
had never been so pitilessly emphasized. Accustomed as we are to

attributing meaning to sound even when it has none, we don't adopt
the ironic distance from it that we do with sight. Here words dis-
port themselves with grotesque immodesty, stripped of the social complicity which clothed them with an illusory dignity. You imagine you
are seeing some words coming out of the radio like a string of red
balloons while others crystallize as little clouds above peoples'
heads and bob about in the wind until they pop up under your nose.
But the worst thing is that they have precisely the meaning that sus-
tained attention finally restores to them as you strain, eyes closed,
to eliminate random noises. Then Tati surreptitiously introduces a
totally irrelevant sound and—tangled up as we are in this sound
skein—we don't even think to protest. It is like the sound effects
of fireworks in which one cannot, without a conscious effort, identify
the sound of a bombing. It's the sound which gives M. Hulot's universe its depth, its moral prominence. Ask yourself where that overwhelming sadness, that inordinate disenchantment comes from at the
end of the film, and you may find that it comes from silence. Throughout the film, the playful cries of children inevitably accompany shots
of the beach, and their abrupt silence signifies the end of the holiday.

M. Hulot, alone, ignored by his hotel companions who will not
forgive him for having spoiled their fireworks display, turns toward
two urchins and engages briefly in a sand battle with them. But surreptitiously a few friends come to say goodbye to him: the old
English woman who keeps score in tennis, the child of the man on the
telephone, the strolling husband . . . the ones, among this rabble
chained to its holiday, in whom there survived a tiny flame of freedom or poetry. The supreme delicacy of this unresolved ending is not
unworthy of the best Chaplin.

As in every great comedy, the comedy of Les Vacances de Monsieur
Hulot is the result of cruel observation. Une si jolie petite plage
of Yves Allegret and Jacques Sigurd seems inspired by a child's primer
in comparison with Tati's film. It does not seem—and that is perhaps
the surest guarantee of its greatness—that Jacques Tati's comedy is
pessimistic, at least no more so than Chaplin's. His character af-
firms, against the world's stupidity, an incorrigible lightness; it
is the proof that the unexpected can still happen, can trouble the
imbeciles' order, transforming an inner tube into a funeral wreath
and a burial into a pleasure trip.

Author Index

Note: The author index covers all of Chapter IV and Tati's writings and interviews in Chapter V.

Author Index

Film Title Index

Note: The film title index covers Chapters III–VII. Entries for Tati's films are listed under their French titles. References to other films are listed as they appear in the text. The category of "Tati's Films--General" includes articles dealing either with several of his films or with his larger oeuvre.

211, 213, 224–225, 227, 233–
234, 240, 249–250, 252–253,
255–259, 262–264, 272, 276–
277, 291, 301, 304, 306,
309, 319, 323–325, 327, 329,
330–333, 335, 341, 353, 401–
406, 410–411, 413, 422–423,
427, 429–430, 445, 452, 459,
462, 464, 466

Recreation, 157. See also
     Playtime.
Red Desert, 183
Retour à la terre, 5, 346, 437

Soigne ton gauche, 4, 78, 345,
     437–438
Sylvie and the Phantom. See
     Sylvie et la fantôme.
Sylvie et la fantôme, 109, 347,
     432, 435, 437–438, 455, 461

Tati's Films--General, 30–31,
     48–49. 51, 57, 59, 61–63,
     66–67, 71–72, 75–76, 78, 81,
     95, 108–109, 115, 123, 126,
     132, 142, 144, 147, 150, 152,
     158, 162, 181, 188, 191–193,
     198, 201, 203–208, 211–213,
     220, 225, 233, 240, 245, 248,
     256–257, 260, 263, 272, 278,
     289, 292, 297, 301, 306–309,
     312, 317, 319, 321, 326,
     328–332, 334, 337–340, 363,
     366, 369, 375, 377, 379, 382,
     388, 391–392, 397, 408, 411,
     414, 421–423, 426–430
Traffic. See Trafic.
Trafic, 11, 209, 211–219, 221–
     224, 226–234, 237–244, 246–
     247, 251, 254, 257, 261, 263,
     265, 267–268, 306, 319, 338,
     354, 418, 420, 423–424, 427,
     437, 439, 452, 465–466
Two or Three Things I Know About
     Her, 183, 240

Les Vacances de Monsieur Hulot,
     1, 8, 24–26, 28–29, 31–32,
     33, 35, 37–43, 45–49, 51–60,
     62–64, 67, 70, 99, 109, 115,

144, 148–149, 151, 153, 159,
188, 191, 198, 203, 213, 225,
246, 257, 295, 301, 303, 305–
307, 313, 315–316, 319, 329,
351, 362, 372, 375, 411, 427,
438–440, 442–443, 457, 459–
460, 462–464, 466

Weekend, 214, 233, 240, 244